PRAISES FOR
RISE OF THE REVENUE

Best marketing book I have read and I have reviewed more than 100 through the years. This book's mandate sets the stage for the future of marketing with Revenue Marketers being the generators of wealth. Presidents must read it to understand what is possible. Sales managers must read it to understand how to lower sales expense and increase sales with less manpower. Marketers must read it to understand what is expected of them. This is not a theory book; it is a book filled with facts from senior marketing managers who have walked the talk and become generators of wealth equal to sales. This is a Sales Lead Management Association recommended book.

– James Obermayer, President of Sales Lead Management Association and Sales Leakage Consulting

Debbie Qaqish uses the voices of real-world marketers to finally put the nonsensical blame game between marketing and sales to rest. In *Rise of the Revenue Marketer*, she explains the dynamic shift of marketing from a cost center to a revenue center. This should be required reading for all sales and marketing professionals seeking to advance their organizations while advancing their careers.

– Paul Nolan, Editor, Sales & Marketing Management

Marketers are now under fire to deliver top-line revenue growth and ROI. But how to do it is the big challenge. In this book, Qaqish offers a playbook for driving this change initiative. It's filled with stories, models, and best practices from a wide variety of companies who've successfully made the transition. *Rise of the Revenue Marketer* also provides a tangible way for sales and marketing to align and create synergies that impact company performance. A must-read for the VP of Sales as well as the VP of Marketing.

– Jill Konrath, President, Fresh Sales Strategies

Barriers between sales and marketing are finally coming down, and the relationship is becoming legitimized. The most successful companies on the planet now recognize the need for harmony and are thriving as a consequence. Debbie's book is unique because it is one of the few with a marketing orientation that makes sense to salespeople. She demonstrates her very wide commercial bandwidth and sophisticated writing skills by producing a masterpiece that resonates across the sales/marketing divide.

– Jonathan Farrington, Senior Partner at Jonathan Farrington & Associates
and CEO of Top Sales World

What's the return on investment for the four bucks you'll spend on this e-book if you're a B2B marketer? Not even worthwhile trying to imagine it. There's a new day dawning for B2B marketing people, and Debbie Qaqish is ringing the wake-up bell. If your boss isn't already asking you what your salary's worth to him in revenue (beyond snappy brochures and kickin' trade show booths), he or she soon will be. You can do two things right now: brush up your résumé or read this book. Qaqish invented the term "revenue marketing," and she sets out what it means for you in no-nonsense fashion. So you can spend four bucks at Starbucks today or you can buy this book. Or you can do both while you still have that high-paying marketing job, and you may even be able to keep it.

– Alan Urbanski, Senior Editor, DMNews

Rise of the Revenue Marketer is an easy read that provides insight and lessons learned from experienced marketing executives. If you're looking for a book that provides step-by-step insights into marketing automation, then this is a great book to check out. Bravo!

– Jamie Turner, CEO of 60 Second Communications, Founder of 60 Second Marketer,
Co-Author *How to Make Money with Social Media* and *Go Mobile*

RISE OF THE REVENUE MARKETER

AN EXECUTIVE PLAYBOOK

RISE OF THE REVENUE MARKETER

AN EXECUTIVE PLAYBOOK

Debbie Qaqish

The Pedowitz Group

Alpharetta, GA

**BOOK**LOGIX®
Alpharetta, GA

BookLogix softcover edition September 2013

ISBN: 978-1-61005-407-2
LCCN: 2013915394

(For information about bulk purchases, please contact the publisher.)

10 9 8 7 6 5 4 3 2   0 9 3 0 1 3

Printed in the United States of America

∞ This paper meets the requirements of ANSI/NISO Z39.48-1992 (Permanence of Paper)

REVENUE MARKETING IS THE STRATEGY THAT TRANSFORMS MARKETING FROM A COST CENTER TO A REVENUE CENTER.

CONTENTS

PREFACE

Every day, I get up loving what I do.

I'm in a fast-growing and innovative space, and I get to work with some of the most phenomenal revenue marketers on the planet. These people with whom I work and interact are true pioneers and are leading important changes in this exciting marketing category called Revenue Marketing. How many people are so lucky?

This book is for them, about them, and thanks to them. More specifically, I wrote this book for the B2B marketing executive who is responsible for:

- identifying, creating, and executing a Revenue Marketing strategy;

- demonstrating direct revenue results and a realistic ROI; and

- transforming marketing from a cost center to a revenue center.

Today's B2B marketing executive is working in a world that is changing faster than the pace at which marketing can adjust. New technologies such as marketing automation have dramatically changed the role of marketing in the revenue equation. Marketing leaders need to effectively and quickly embrace and optimize these new dynamics.

As I am watching this market mature, I see plenty of education for marketers at the tactical level. What I don't see is education, best practices, or even a basic playbook written just for the executive Revenue Marketer. A playbook that marketing leaders can use to move revenue marketing from an innovative strategy to a well-executed, multifaceted, and multi-year plan for transforming marketing.

This book is such a Playbook. What you won't see is a list of Top 5 email best practices or Top 10 ways to improve campaign effectiveness. This is not a tactical book. What you will see is a set of revenue marketing plays (stories, best practices, models, and frameworks) developed from:

- my own experiences working with hundreds of sales and marketing executives,

- my company's experiences working with over 1,100 sales and marketing organizations, and

- recent interviews I conducted with twenty-four experienced executive-level Revenue Marketers.

I think you'll love, connect with, and learn from their stories.

I personally understand the frustration of not knowing how to execute a revenue marketing strategy and get to the revenue results promised to your company. As the VP of marketing for a software company, I purchased my first marketing automation system in 2005 and promised my CEO a home run. I quickly found that it wasn't that simple. In 2005, there were no benchmarks for revenue marketing because revenue marketing was not even a concept.

I was a leader, and I was lost. It didn't feel good to be in a leadership position and not know what to do. I did not need training on the software—my team could get that. I needed help with all of the other things that make up revenue marketing—people, process, change management, and strategy execution. I didn't know what I didn't know.

I called Eloqua and asked their CEO for help. He put me in touch with their VP of professional services, Jeff Pedowitz. Jeff helped me figure out my strategy and how to execute. Based on that strategy, my marketing group and I returned a year one ROI of 20:1 on our investment and completely transformed the role of marketing in revenue at our company. From this engagement, Jeff and I discovered a common passion for the space and decided to begin new careers. Jeff started The Pedowitz Group in 2007, and I joined a few months later.

Whether you are a marketing leader at the beginning of your revenue marketing journey, a leader who wants to speed up and optimize your current journey, or if you are just interested in learning more about the innovation of revenue marketing and how to do it, you have come to the right place.

On a personal note, I would like to thank the people who have helped me and without whom this book would never have made it to print.

First and foremost, I want to thank my friend and business partner, Jeff Pedowitz, for sharing the vision and allowing me to take time away from the business at a critical juncture in our growth to complete this book.

I also would like to thank all of the revenue marketers who participated in the interview process for this book. They shared their experiences along their journeys and added so much to these revenue marketing plays including Cleve Bellar, Dianne Conley, Rachel Dennis, Andrew Devlin, Kristen Diamond, Lawrence DiCapua, Doug Fogwell, Patty Foley-Reid, Nancy Harris, Amy Hawthorne, Laura Hoffman, Jim Kanir, Sally Lowery, Liz McClellan, Chris Newton, Fiona Nolan, Alex Pelletier, Jeff Ramminger, Ken Robinson, Shawnn Smark, Eva Tsai, Joseph Vesey, Evan Whitenight, and Kristen Wright. They represent a cross section of companies based on industry and size.

I would also like to thank Cathy Johnson, copy editor and good friend, whose attention to detail and patience kept me sane and ultimately helped to make this book a reality.

"The other day, Deron Frye, SVP of sales, said to me, 'You guys are just a different breed of marketer than I am used to. You approach things much more scientifically, and it's the first time I've ever heard marketing talk about true, metric-driven programs.' I laughed and told him that's because we're Revenue Marketers. Get used to this!"

– Liz McClellan, VP of Field Marketing for PGi

"Revenue marketing is a way to make our business more profitable, efficient, and effective, and it will help us compete in the marketplace. Across our dozens of competitors, I am sure there are others who are probably thinking the same thing, and if they don't move forward, they will be left behind."

– Lawrence DiCapua, Leader of GE's Revenue Marketing Center of Excellence

"I am energized and intrigued by the marriage of sales and marketing and the greater role that marketing can take in an organization. Marketing has been traditionally viewed as a 'nice to have'—they make things pretty, they have fun parties. But it's time for B2B marketers to look at the sales funnel and proactively decide if they want to be part of the next level of marketing. When I first heard the term revenue marketing, I thought—*Yes! That's it!*"

– Laura Hoffman, VP of Global Marketing at Red Lion Controls

1

WHAT ARE YOU GOING TO DO ABOUT REVENUE?

"So, Debbie, what are *you* going to do about revenue?"

Several years ago, while VP of marketing for an Atlanta software firm, my CEO walked into my office one morning and confronted me with this bombshell of a question.

My first thought was, *It says VP of marketing on the door—not VP of sales!*

Like many companies, top-line revenue growth and profit were business imperatives for us, and it had become clear in the last few years that simply adding more salespeople as a path to revenue growth was just not going to cut it.

Keep in mind that this wasn't my first rodeo. Prior to joining this particular firm, I had been a VP of sales for many years, and our CEO was doing what good CEOs do best—pushing each member of the executive team to think outside the box and look for new solutions to the age-old problem of revenue production. Given my sales background, my CEO was asking me to look at marketing from a new angle—a *revenue* angle.

As a former VP of sales, I was accustomed to talking about revenue. Throughout all of those years in sales and leading sales teams, I had never asked myself how marketing might directly impact revenue and—moreover—how to track the metrics to *prove* that it did. For me, it had always been about acquiring qualified leads with little help from marketing. Marketing was the creative side, the "make it pretty" department. I honestly didn't care what font or color was being used on the website. I had a sales team to run, and we had a number to hit!

My personal experience with marketing had very little to do with revenue production—that was the sole domain of sales and, frankly, marketing was not my problem. And it certainly wasn't the answer.

But all of that changed when I took the role of VP of marketing and my CEO asked me *The Question*. My perception of marketing as not being a direct revenue contributor went up in smoke, and my journey to becoming a revenue marketer began.

Immediately, I went into investigative mode.

I searched for experts, asking them what marketers can do about revenue, and soon became engaged with a classification of tools called marketing automation. I still remember the meeting, the people, the room, and even the date of my first marketing automation capabilities presentation.

I was blown away. I instantly knew it had the potential to totally change how I was running my marketing organization and the role marketing would play in driving revenue. I thought to myself, *This is going to dramatically change the relationship between sales and marketing, redefine how revenue is driven, and help me answer my CEO's challenge.*

Marketing Gets a Seat at the Revenue Table

– Liz McClellan, VP of Field Marketing, PGi

Marketing hasn't always had a seat at the revenue table at Premiere Global Services (PGi), a worldwide provider of conferencing and collaboration solutions. Marketing was known for producing great graphics, buying lists, and sending direct mail campaigns, but this wasn't producing the results needed to grow the company.

PGi wanted to move marketing from its traditional role to a revenue center. Marketing had not been held accountable for revenue results in the past and knew they needed to earn credibility.

When Liz McClellan came on board, she began to reeducate the organization. She immediately started working hand in hand with sales to transition marketing from working with unqualified suspects to a process where they could better qualify and nurture leads into true prospects, and then hand truly qualified leads over to sales.

Liz included metrics in every conversation, as she challenged sales executives to imagine a better world where sales spent less time hunting and more time closing. She convinced leadership that, instead of increasing sales headcount, marketing would enable sales to be vastly more productive.

"We got their attention because we talked to them about things they could relate to, about how we would move the needle from the top of the funnel to closed sales," said Liz, VP of field marketing at PGi. "We discussed the difference between suspects, prospects, and leads. Right up front, I told them that what they had been calling a 'lead' wasn't really a lead."

An infrastructure for a tightly integrated sales and marketing team was put in place over several months. At a recent sales kick-off with 400 people, Marc Lambert, SVP of sales, turned to Liz and said, "I now totally get what you were saying. The answer isn't necessarily about adding more headcount. It's about building the proper infrastructure to make our existing reps more productive. I support you 100 percent."

RISE OF THE REVENUE MARKETER

Fast forward to 2007. As a principal at The Pedowitz Group, I spent a lot of time doing webinars and speaking to marketing groups about marketing automation and related topics. As early as 2008, I began asking these groups my version of *The Question*: **Who has some kind of responsibility for revenue? And, if you don't, do you think it's coming soon?**

Since 2008, the answers to those questions have changed. Here's the general evolution:

- **2008** – Everyone was pretty uncomfortable with this question! Maybe 10 percent raised their hands.
- **2009** – 15 percent raised their hands, but they were still uncomfortable.
- **2010** – 25 percent were braver and raised their hands, but many still acted as if they needed therapy. It was still a fairly new concept!
- **2011** – 50 percent of marketers were now proud to raise their hands.
- **2012** – 70 percent raised their hands. Those marketers who did not raise their hands were now beginning to feel left out and behind the curve.
- **2013** – Today, about 70 percent are still raising their hands, but we now have a new classification of "serial revenue marketers" who have taken the revenue marketing journey with more than one company.

Over time, we began to see more and more B2B marketers playing a direct and significant role in revenue. We began to think that this new kind of marketing not only needed a new name, but a distinct definition as well.

Our first thought was, let's call this "smarketing" because it's really a mash-up of sales and marketing. But all I could think of was those little blue Smurfs. We also thought about "smarketeers," but that was a little too Disney-like. Finally, in 2010, we came up with the term Revenue Marketing, and wow, did it make sense!

Immediate Identification

– Amy Hawthorne, B2B Revenue Marketing Leader at Rackspace

"The first time I heard the term *Revenue Marketing*, I immediately identified myself as a revenue marketer. A business just can't run at its full potential without strategic revenue marketing."

When we first used the term, we'd see a client's eyes light up with interest, and then we knew we had a good prospect for our services. For those marketers who looked at us as though we had sprouted a second head, we knew they would probably *not* be a good prospect for us. The term helped us identify potential and like-minded clients who were ready to make a change and who were open to marketing's new role in revenue.

We began using the term Revenue Marketing and Revenue Marketer in 2010 when this space was still called many different things, from "lead management" to "marketing automation" and even "demand generation." We liked the term so much and thought it was so relevant to the market that we trademarked it. Today, the term Revenue Marketing has taken on a life of its own with many marketers even using the term as part of their title.

As the market has continued to evolve, our definition of what it means to be a revenue marketer has also evolved:

- **2010** – We began using the term in early 2010 and at that time defined *revenue marketers* as marketers with some kind of revenue accountability. The term *revenue marketing* was an overarching term without a clear and specific definition. It was more of a Big Idea.
- **2011** – In 2011, our definition became much more specific: A Revenue Marketer is a specific type of marketer just like product marketing or marketing communications. Revenue marketers have revenue or revenue-related accountability through the kinds of programs, campaigns, communications, and digital interactions they create. They are responsible for the top of the sales funnel and interacting with and nurturing leads until they are sales ready. They are also responsible for helping to accelerate leads through the sales funnel. They all use some type of marketing automation platform integrated with CRM to power their revenue marketing practice and to achieve revenue results.
- **2012** – In 2012, we added the concept that Revenue Marketing is a strategy designed to transform marketing from a cost center to a revenue center and in that process demonstrate a business ROI. More specifically, revenue marketers are responsible for driving repeatable, predictable, and scalable (RPS) revenue performance. *Repeatable* means that there is a formula. *Predictable* indicates that the VP of marketing can forecast revenue from marketing, and *scalable* means that you can apply revenue marketing to any magnitude and achieve a predictable return.

REVENUE MARKETING DEFINED

The combined set of strategies, processes, people, technologies, content, and results across marketing and sales that does four things:

Drops sales-ready leads into the top of the funnel.

Accelerates sales opportunities through the sales pipeline.

Measures marketing based on repeatable, predictable, and scalable (RPS) contribution to pipeline, revenue, and ROI.

Transforms marketing from a cost center to a revenue center.

That's It!

– Laura Hoffman, VP of Global Marketing at Red Lion Controls

"I am energized and intrigued by the marriage of sales and marketing and the greater role that marketing can take in an organization. Marketing has been traditionally viewed as a 'nice to have' – they make things pretty, they have fun parties. But it's time for B to B marketers to look at the sales funnel and proactively decide if they want to be part of the next level of marketing. When I first heard the term *revenue marketing*, I thought – Yes! That's it!"

It has been many years since my CEO first asked me how I planned to contribute to revenue, and a lot has changed since then. In today's economic environment, C-level executives are focused on revenue, and savvy executives expect more from their marketing teams—and not just more activity. They expect a direct revenue impact. Across the board, these executives want a *measurable return on their marketing investment*—a direct connection between marketing activities and closed business. They want *proof* that marketing is making a real impact on revenue.

- Today's **CEO** is asking, *How can marketing more effectively help grow our company in markets with ever-increasing competition?*

- Today's **CFO** is asking, *What revenue impact is marketing making, and what's the ROI?*

- Today's **COO** is asking, *How can marketing help increase operational efficiency and effectiveness in the marketing and sales process?*

- Today's **VP of Sales** is asking, *How can marketing help us find substantially more sales-ready leads? How can we get to these leads before the competition, and how can we get opportunities through the sales funnel faster?*

All of this pressure is rolling downhill to the CMO or VP of marketing, who can then look at the situation in one of two ways: 1. the sky is falling (disaster) or 2. there is a silver lining in this cloud (opportunity). Patty Foley-Reid of Iron Mountain and Lawrence DiCapua of GE see it as an opportunity.

Revenue Marketing Machine

– Patty Foley-Reid, Director of Inbound and Content Marketing at Iron Mountain

"The goal of demand generation at Iron Mountain is to be a dependable, strategic revenue lever for the business. In other words, a Revenue Marketing machine. We want to reach the point where it is understood that when you put more money into demand generation, you get a predictable return on your investment."

Revenue Marketing— Why Now?

– Lawrence DiCapua, Leader of GE's Revenue Marketing Center of Excellence

At GE, like many global enterprise companies, the driving force behind adopting revenue marketing was the need to operate more productively and efficiently. But another key driver was the desire to dominate the competition.

"We don't like to be followers—we like to be leaders. And we certainly don't like to respond," said Lawrence DiCapua, leader of GE's Revenue Marketing Center of Excellence. "We want to be the ones who are out there first."

Early in their revenue marketing journey, executives at GE who have become familiar with the power of revenue marketing see it as a real opportunity for growth—both in the marketplace and internally at GE.

"We looked to revenue marketing because we needed more accountability. We needed a better way of measuring the impact of our marketing dollars and a better way to determine how we can improve," said Lawrence. "Revenue marketing really connects marketing investments with outcomes and that's the type of logic that really resonates with senior leaders. And when you start talking about how those investments translate into revenue, now you can have a discussion about what's working, what is not, and how to improve."

WHAT CHANGED?

Prior to the pervasive use of the Internet (I know this goes *way* back in time, but it's important!), if a client or prospect wanted to learn about your solutions, they picked up the phone and called you. A meeting would be arranged, and your sales team would trot out to do their pitch—along with five other companies in the running. In this model, sales was actively involved from the very *beginning* of the buyer's journey and in every subsequent step. Figure 1.1 represents how sales was involved in the buyer journey pre-Internet.

PRE-INTERNET SALES INVOLVEMENT IN THE BUYER'S JOURNEY

Figure 1.1

In comes the Internet. Buyers are now no longer calling sales as they begin their journey. Instead, they are going online to gather the information they need. Salespeople have lost critical visibility into buyer behavior, and there is a huge information and communication gap between sales activities and what the buyer is actually doing.

Analysts with Corporate Executive Board and Sirius Decisions report that today's buyers are typically anywhere from 60–70 percent through their buyer journey before a company is even aware that there is an opportunity. Figure 1.2 represents how sales is involved post the Internet and the resulting gap.

Who is addressing this gap? (And it's a BIG gap.)

WHO IS ADDRESSING THIS GAP?

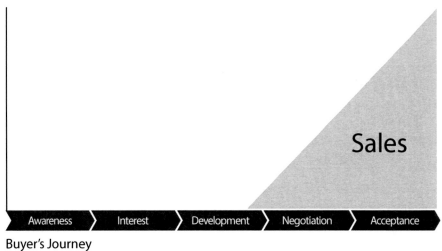

Figure 1.2

With the rapid rise in the use of marketing automation technologies, this responsibility now falls to marketing. And in a revenue marketing paradigm, marketing's role does not end once a qualified lead is passed over. At this point, marketing's job is only half done. Revenue marketers are also responsible for working with sales to develop and deploy tactics and strategies to stop lead leakage, improve conversions, and close more business, in less time and with a higher average order size. In essence, marketing and sales are now working together to create a *single and predictable revenue continuum*. Figure 1.3 represents the new role for marketing.

NEW ROLE FOR MARKETING

Figure 1.3

In this new model, marketing's key role will be providing behavioral intelligence to sales.

Marketing Provides
Behavioral Intelligence

– Jeff Ramminger, Senior Vice President of Field Marketing & Client Consulting at TechTarget

"How much behavioral intelligence you can deliver to a salesperson is going to differentiate the conversation they can have *and should have* with the prospect. Smart salespeople are really going to embrace that and want a tremendous amount of knowledge about the prospect before they ever interact with them. In the revenue marketing journey, the most successful revenue marketers are going to be the best internal salespeople, convincing the sales team that sales has changed dramatically and is never going back to the way it was."

Bowling Behind the Curtain

– Jim Kanir, SVP of Sales and Marketing at Billtrust

Jim Kanir, SVP of sales and marketing at Billtrust, a billing services provider, looks at marketing automation as the paradigm shift in revenue marketing.

"In the old days, marketing just put content out there, and I like to compare it to bowling with a curtain across the pins," said Jim. "We rolled the ball down the aisle and could hear that some pins were knocked down, but we couldn't tell how many, which pins, or if we were getting a strike or not. Today, marketing uses digital insight, which is comparable to removing the curtain. Now we roll the ball down the aisle and can actually see what pins are going down and what the interaction is between the pins. Did we knock a few down? Get a strike? Do we adjust our approach?" With marketing automation, we now have the visibility we need.

OTHER RESEARCH

What other evidence do we have that the role of marketing is changing? A recent study from IBM called "Stretched to Strengthened, Insights from the Global Chief Marketing Officer Study" interviewed 1,700 CMOs from around the globe. The most telling data from this report is represented in Figure 1.4. CMOs in this study reported that their *number one metric for the future will be marketing ROI.* An interesting thing about ROI is—last time I checked—that you can't calculate ROI without *revenue*. In fact, third through sixth place on CMOs' list of priorities are all related to revenue.

HOW CMOs WILL BE MEASURED

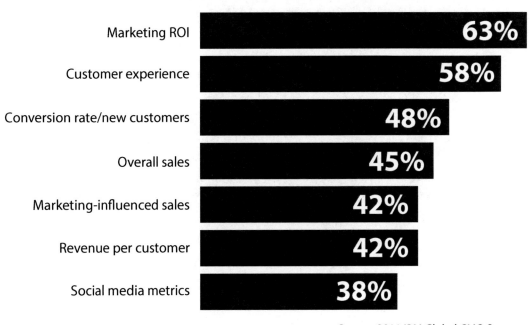

Marketing ROI	63%
Customer experience	58%
Conversion rate/new customers	48%
Overall sales	45%
Marketing-influenced sales	42%
Revenue per customer	42%
Social media metrics	38%

Source: 2011 IBM Global CMO Survey

Figure 1.4

The Building Block Approach to Revenue Marketing

– Ken Robinson, VP of Revenue Marketing, NAVEX Global

ELT, a trusted ethics and compliance expert, had an aggressive growth strategy. After acquiring three different companies in 2012, they began doing business as NAVEX Global.

However, when Ken Robinson joined ELT, it was a forty-person company backed by a private equity organization. ELT wanted a more progressive marketing approach and knew they needed to build an infrastructure so marketing could move from being a cost center to a revenue center for the business. ELT also needed more insight from marketing into what was going on in the mid-part of their funnel and wanted to see higher conversion rates and lead velocity.

To facilitate the changes, ELT wanted a seasoned marketing executive with marketing automation (MA) expertise who was familiar with closed-loop sales and marketing processes and had a proven track record of driving revenue.

Ken joined ELT as VP of revenue marketing and quickly painted a vision for the executive team, including the CEO and president, the VP of sales, and the board of directors, on how things can and should be. Ken came in with a playbook—a building block approach for how they could get there with the right technology, programs, people, and process.

"I had worked in this area for years and had been a part of one of the first fifty or so companies to implement marketing automation with Marketo. We were one of the early adopters, so I had really cut my teeth on this type of technology and overall marketing approach," said Ken.

Within three months, marketing automation was operational and in six months, a solid foundation was built. By nine months, marketing was using advanced MA techniques.

"I started with sales and marketing alignment on very basic lead scoring, profiling, and nurturing, then moved to much more advanced things. Within a year, we were using more predictive analytics, historical data on where the business had been, and identifying conversion rates and key input variables," Ken said.

Then came the mergers, with the purchase of three different companies over six months. Ken observed many of the same challenges that he'd seen at ELT. Marketing was measuring impact and performance based on vanity metrics but wasn't committed to driving a percentage of net new revenue. In addition, there was no alignment between sales and marketing, leads were simply thrown over the fence to sales, and there was no transparency from a reporting perspective. His work was cut out for him to bring them all together as one organization.

"The good news was they had an idea of where they wanted to go, but they hadn't had the expertise on staff to actually build that out," said Ken. "Since I had already done this for ELT, I had total support at the executive level. I was put forth as a person who could take what we had done when we were only 40 people and do this again for an organization that is now 500 people doing business globally."

Sales leadership also backed him fully. "I had enough people who said, 'Ken can deliver on these promises. He's got a vision, he knows where he's going, he knows how to get there, and he will deliver results along the way,'" Ken said.

Ken was careful to set expectations that the revenue marketing journey can take eighteen months to several years but guaranteed that they would show incremental progress and see changes along the way. For example, they've implemented better campaign reporting for more accurate revenue attribution. Metrics are now more trustworthy, data is more granular, and they have better reporting at both the territory and account level.

Ken's team started with two people at ELT and has grown to a revenue marketing team of twenty-two people, including a business analyst, a marketing technologist, and a senior demand generation marketer.

"It's a marathon, it's not a sprint. But we built a solid foundation over twelve months, beginning at ELT and scaling that as we grew into NAVEX Global. Now we're looking for better results and ways to optimize our people, processes, and technology. Across the organization, we are now recognized as the revenue marketing team, not just marketing."

KEY PLAY

You only have one Key Play at this point.

1. Take the initiative to understand more about Revenue Marketing and determine if this is a strategy for your company and your career. Begin by answering these questions:

- What am I going to do about revenue?

- Is what I'm doing as a marketing leader good enough?

- What are my peers in my industry doing?

- What is happening in my organization and in my industry?

- Do I need to change the status quo?

I have found that the Revenue Marketing Journey doesn't happen overnight, and there are many variables as to how long a company's journey will actually take based on things like politics, red tape, and urgency. At Pinstripe, we had such an aptitude for change, a passion for technology, and openness to what's best in class that everyone was keen to accelerate and start filling the pipeline with new leads. I've been in a different organization that was bigger and less agile and I know how you can get hung up, even if you have the best will and finest team in the world. If you've got all of the internal stuff to work through, it can take a lot longer. But even with the right culture, alignment, and support, I would say it's still at least a two-year journey to where you have a repeatable, predictable, and scalable revenue marketing model.

– Kristen Wright, VP of Marketing at Pinstripe

This is a journey, and no single journey will be the same because there are going to be different influencing factors. You have to find your own way, but gather as much information as you can from other people who have been through it. Reaching out is a very sensible and strategic thing to do because you will learn so much.

**– Rachel Dennis, Director of Lead Generation
and Retention at Getty Images**

To be successful on this journey, we can't have a 'not invented here' mentality. We must be competitive, we must continue to learn, and we must continue to socialize the new role of marketing in driving revenue.

**– Joseph Vesey, Chief Marketing Officer at
Xylem, Inc.**

2

THE REVENUE MARKETING JOURNEY

It's two a.m., and I'm in a hotel room in Austin, Texas, working on my second pot of coffee and preparing for the first of fourteen Revenue Rockstar events sponsored by Marketo.

We start bright and early at eight thirty, and I'm the lead-off speaker. My job is to set the tone for the day's conversation and frame-up both the market and how to become a Revenue Marketer.

I had been noodling around an idea for a simple four-stage journey and decided I'd take a risk and test the idea during this road show. I figured this was a great stage for testing and honing the idea (if it worked) and the message.

As I was introduced as the first speaker, my palms were sweating and my heart was pounding. Was I about to lose all credibility or would this simple framework make sense to this marketing audience?

I began my presentation, introduced the model (see fig. 2.1), and carefully watched the audience. I saw them sitting straight, intently watching the big screen. They were nodding their heads in agreement and furiously scribbling down notes.

THE PEDOWITZ GROUP
THE REVENUE MARKETING JOURNEY

| Traditional | Lead Generation | Demand Generation | Revenue Marketing |

Figure 2.1

As I finished my presentation, I felt the four-stage Revenue Marketing Journey (RMJ) had been well received, but the best was yet to come. The speaker after me immediately incorporated the RMJ stages into *his* talk. Even better, when all of the presentations were over and I began to meet and talk with different members of the audience, marketers began using the same terminology in their conversations! "Debbie, we're late in the lead generation stage," or "Debbie, we've just begun the demand generation stage…"

Marketers at all different levels got it instantly. It made sense to the VPs, and it made sense to the managers. It provided a road map to show them where they were today and gave them a vision and direction for where they needed to be—and that end state was revenue marketing.

I presented and discussed the Revenue Marketing Journey at all fourteen live events around the county to thousands of marketers on that road show, and the response was universally the same in every city. Since 2011, we've continued to hone this model, and it continues to help marketers set a vision and a path to achieving that vision.

Today, we have a much better rendering of the RMJ, and it is the foundation we use in every customer engagement (see fig. 2.2).

THE PEDOWITZ GROUP
REVENUE MARKETING JOURNEY

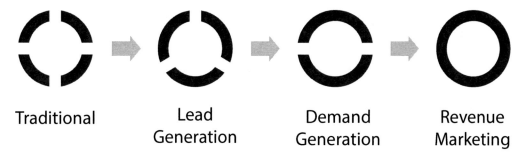

| Traditional | Lead Generation | Demand Generation | Revenue Marketing |

Figure 2.2

WE WANT TO START THE REVENUE MARKETING JOURNEY *NOW*

Our CEO, Jeff Pedowitz, was recently invited to participate as part of a vendor's marketing automation demo. His role was to listen in and present one token slide about The Pedowitz Group's services in the presentation. The company was a large global conglomerate, and the VP of marketing was in the audience.

After the introductions, Jeff was to present his one slide and then the vendor was to provide a high-level overview of their software. That software overview never happened.

Once Jeff presented the Revenue Marketing Journey slide, the VP engaged in a fifty-minute conversation around the journey and ended the conversation with, "We're ready to get started on this journey right now!"

THE REVENUE MARKETING JOURNEY MODEL

The Revenue Marketing Journey model presents four distinct stages to achieving revenue marketing status: Traditional, Lead Generation, Demand Generation, and finally, Revenue Marketing, the stage in which marketing has transformed from a cost center to a revenue center.

Stage #1: Traditional Marketing

REVENUE MARKETING JOURNEY

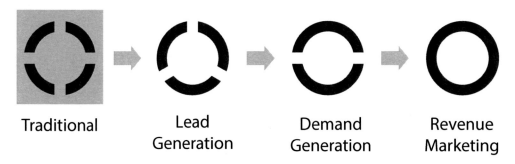

Traditional   Lead Generation   Demand Generation   Revenue Marketing

As a seasoned executive marketer, you probably don't need much explanation of what traditional marketing entails. Characterized by the Four Ps—*Product, Promotion, Placement,* and *Price*—traditional marketing is what is taught in undergraduate and graduate programs and what most marketers experience every day. For many B2B marketing organizations at this stage, marketing has little political clout, does not have a seat at the revenue table, and is seen as the "make it pretty" department. Senior executives in this organization don't even realize the revenue impact marketing *could* make on top-line revenue growth.

Traditional marketers are focused on creating and implementing marketing strategies and tactics without true insight into the impact of those initiatives. They typically report on a host of **activity-based metrics** such as number of ads, number of impressions, number of attendees to an event, and number of visits. For many companies, it is largely a blind spend, representing a huge budget and providing metrics that key executives don't really care about.

Nearly every B2B company leverages elements of traditional marketing, and we estimate that 50 percent of the market is in this stage of the Revenue Marketing Journey.

Marketing executives are looking beyond traditional marketing for a more relevant and effective way of marketing—one that eventually earns marketing a seat at the revenue table. These next three phases include defining characteristics and key metrics. Pay special attention to these metrics as they change over the course of the journey. And remember, what gets measured, gets done!

Read how Joseph Vesey of Xylem is transforming marketing from traditional marketers to revenue marketers.

Marketing as a Line Function
– Joseph Vesey, Chief Marketing Officer, Xylem, Inc.

"In the past, marketing has not generated enough leads outside of traditional tradeshows. We didn't generate leads that created demand," said Joseph Vesey, chief marketing officer at Xylem, Inc.

"We're fast changing our traditional, ineffective marketing approach to one in which marketing is a line function, where our mission is to acquire, grow, and retain."

A line function, like sales and manufacturing, is business critical to the everyday operation of a company. If it goes down, it has an immediate impact on the company and the customer.

"Having marketing as a line function is a vision, and we're not there yet," said Joseph. "This means I want to take more things in-house. I want to scale it across our business and the industry. Half of our revenue goes to our channel partners. I want to be a holistic lead generator for that business so that if I turned it off, they would immediately become dissatisfied. That qualifies us as a line function and gives us power in the market. That's where marketing plays offense."

Marketing at Xylem kicked off a multi-year plan where, as skills and capabilities are built, they will become a revenue generator with accountability to the company and channel partners.

"Today, we are talking about generating leads. Next year, we won't have a lead number, we'll have a revenue number," Joseph said. "W e'll identify processes and the funnel realization rate so we know what marketing activities and leads are generating revenue."

Stage #2: Lead Generation

REVENUE MARKETING JOURNEY

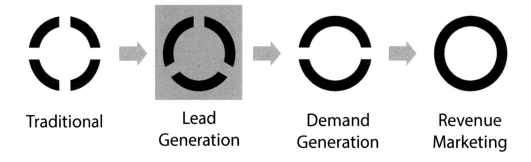

Traditional   Lead Generation   Demand Generation   Revenue Marketing

The first big step towards revenue marketing is making the transition from traditional marketing to lead generation marketing.

Lead generation marketing is characterized by one major goal: providing leads to sales. At this stage of the Revenue Marketing Journey, marketing has acquired an e-mail system and is busy sending one-off e-mails to as many people as possible. These tactical activities produce "leads" (any prospect with a pulse) that are then sent to sales.

The expectation is that sales will pounce on these leads immediately and convert them to opportunities. Instead, what we typically see at this stage is a "cold war" between marketing and sales. Marketing feels they are working hard to acquire leads that sales simply ignore. At the same time, sales feels the leads provided by marketing aren't worth the effort. Just because someone opened an e-mail or downloaded a white paper does not mean they are ready to buy or even ready to talk to sales!

Even if sales does follow up, the visibility into what happens to a lead passed from marketing is not available because an automated, closed-loop system like marketing automation plus CRM is not in place. The lead "leaks" out of the system and both marketing and sales have no appreciation, view, or tools to take advantage of a larger set of possibilities.

After a few years of this kind of behavior, the "cold war" is in full force and neither team respects the other. Marketing is still considered a cost center, and the alignment with sales is neither productive nor collaborative.

Key metrics at this stage are activity-based and generally include number of e-mails sent, open rate, click-through rate, number of forms submitted, percentage of forms completed, number of leads sent to sales, and cost per lead. Once a lead is passed on to sales, marketing's job is complete.

Marketers at this stage are moving in the right direction, but are still viewed as a cost center to the organization.

We estimate that 25 percent of the market is at the Lead Generation stage of the journey. This number may sound low, but we see many companies who have an e-mail system, but are not actively generating leads for sales. Instead, they are using their e-mail systems to generate awareness and to run general communication campaigns.

Stage #3: Demand Generation

REVENUE MARKETING JOURNEY

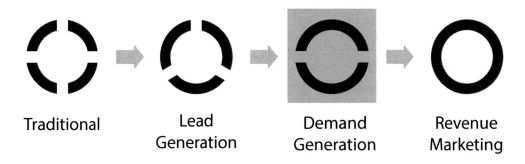

| Traditional | Lead Generation | Demand Generation | Revenue Marketing |

The move from lead generation to demand generation is a strategic leap for most organizations. At this stage, we see the implementation of a full-featured marketing automation system integrated with CRM as the technical backbone. This architecture allows for an automated, closed-loop view and reporting system for the first time and ushers in the foundation for a change in marketing's role.

This stage requires strong executive leadership, as many elements from the lead generation stage change drastically. Rather than sending one-off e-mails to the masses, this stage is characterized by targeted and ongoing nurture programs across all phases of the buyer journey.

Marketers now focus on funnel conversions, especially lower in the funnel, and providing sales-ready leads to sales. Their job does not end once a lead is passed to sales. Rather, marketing works with sales to continue the digital dialogue and to better understand and share relevant insights and intelligence on the digital behavior of prospects. As a result, the relationship between sales and marketing begins to improve as key processes, systems, and visibility are put into place.

The metrics tracked in this phase are also significantly different from prior stages, as they change from being activity-based metrics to **revenue-based metrics**. This can be a tricky period, since the marketing team itself can be the biggest barrier to change because they are uncomfortable with revenue accountability.

Results...Not Activities

– Amy Hawthorne, B2B Revenue Marketing Leader at Rackspace

"This is not a sprint. Those of us who have done it before tend to want to make it a sprint because we know what it's like on the other side. We know what is going to come out of the engine once it's built so we want to hurry up and do it, but that doesn't mean it's the right way. This is about results—not activities."

Key metrics in the demand generation stage of the Revenue Marketing Journey include the number of marketing qualified leads (MQLs) sent to sales; the percentage of MQLs sent to sales that convert to opportunities; the percentage of those opportunities that convert to close; the average number of days to close; and marketing's contribution to the overall pipeline. These are the kinds of metrics that transform marketing from a cost center to a revenue center.

During this stage, senior executives begin to better understand the revenue contribution marketing can make. Based on the revenue marketing model, they begin to recalibrate how they view the role of marketing in the revenue discussion. I always tell marketers that this is the stage at which you need to be careful what you wish for, because it's becoming realized. You'll find yourself at another level of revenue accountability. There's no more hiding behind activities and projects.

We estimate that 25 percent of the market is at the Demand Generation stage of the journey.

The Demand Generation stage is a long one, and savvy revenue marketers like Andrew Devlin of Brinker Capital and Fiona Nolan of CommScope understand there is a right way to navigate this stage of the journey.

Executive Buy-In

– Andrew Devlin, Communications Specialist at Brinker Capital

"I think we are well on our way and within the next two years, we're going to be far ahead of our competitors in our outbound marketing and lead nurturing process. We have total buy-in from upper management and from our marketing team. They know this works and everyone wants it right away, but we are taking our time and doing it right."

Managing Change

– Fiona Nolan, SVP Marketing, CommScope

Three years ago, the opportunity to implement a marketing automation system at the communications network company CommScope presented itself to Fiona Nolan, SVP of global marketing, but the timing wasn't right. An acquisition had doubled the company's footprint, and marketing departments, scattered around the globe, were not working in synergy.

Eventually, Fiona acquired all of marketing within the organization, and her first task was to reengineer her expanded marketing team to ensure the right talent was in place for the new role of marketing and revenue. She also began to identify where the highest growth opportunities were and to begin aligning marketing with key sales people in those areas to help champion the initiative. Finding early adopters—people who understood the changing roles of both sales and marketing—would be key to showing quick wins and gaining trust across the organization.

Fiona emphasized the importance of setting realistic expectations and to make leadership aware of the many changes that needed to take place before the final goal would be realized.

"I keep telling my team, you need to preface all of your discussions with, 'This is not something that is going to happen overnight.' We need to be careful of the expectations we are setting. We know what the end game is, but everyone must recognize the change that has to happen in between," said Fiona.

Fiona took over the company's web presence as an integral part of their revenue marketing efforts and began to restructure the team, bringing in new talent with analytical capabilities and other revenue marketing skills. A key role was bringing in a Revenue Marketing Sales managers in various business units came on board as they began to see the competitive advantages in marketing having a revenue number.

"When I thought we were ready, we pushed the button. We're constantly expanding our efforts into new business units and new countries, as they see the results we've achieved. I see our next phase of growth to extend revenue marketing into our partner ecosystem."

Stage #4: Revenue Marketing

REVENUE MARKETING JOURNEY

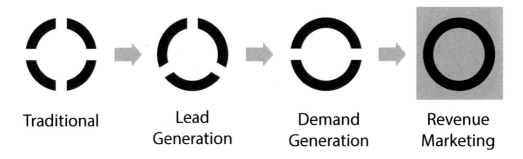

| Traditional | Lead Generation | Demand Generation | Revenue Marketing |

The Revenue Marketing stage includes everything in the demand generation stage with one major difference: the revenue generated and attributed to marketing is now delivered in a machine that is *repeatable*, *predictable*, and *scalable* (RPS).

When the CMO or VP of marketing walks into a senior management team meeting, they come with two different reports. The first is a report showing the revenue contribution from marketing over the past month, quarter, or year. The second, and more powerful, is the Marketing Forecast Report that forecasts revenue impact from marketing for the upcoming period. From the top of the marketing funnel to a booked piece of business, marketing has established conversation rates and can predict revenue outcomes. At this stage, if you give marketing one dollar in additional budget, they can tell you how much revenue will be driven from the additional investment.

Marketing now has a mature revenue marketing practice. How revenue is generated in the company is vastly different from the past. Revenue is now a team effort between marketing and sales. Marketing carries a **"quota"** that aligns with sales goals and marketing is partially compensated on meeting that quota.

Marketing is now a true revenue center.

We estimate that only 5 percent of the market is at this advanced stage.

From Cost Center to Revenue Center

– Sally Lowery, Senior Director of Marketing for Appia

"I don't want to be just a pretty campaign person. When executives look at me, I want them to say, *Sally drives revenue and brings value to this organization.* In my experience, when you walk in and say that you want to own this and want accountability for it, you don't have to spend a lot of time getting buy-in from the field. If you're a marketer who says you want to move marketing from being a cost center to a revenue center, it really evolves the conversation quickly because that's what they want to hear."

To put the entire model into perspective, look at Figure 2.3. The Revenue Marketing Journey detail shows key characteristics and metrics for each stage of the Revenue Marketing Journey.

REVENUE MARKETING JOURNEY DETAIL

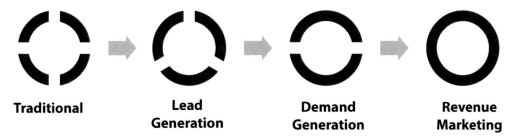

Traditional	Lead Generation	Demand Generation	Revenue Marketing
Cost Center	**Cost Center**	**Cost/Revenue Center**	**Revenue Center**
• The MarCom Group • The *"make it pretty"* department • Marketing focuses on brand building and impressions • No B2B lead generation • No alignment with sales	• E-mail system • Tactical • One-off e-mails centered on generating leads • Focus on the cost of lead generation • Little alignment with sales	• Marketing automation + CRM • Strategic • Nurture MQLs/SALs/SQLs/Opportunities • Marketing funnel • Buyer journey • Full alignment with sales	• Systems are optimized • People and processes are optimized • Repeatable, predictable, scalable (RPS) revenue production • Synergy with sales
Metrics: Accountable for costs and activities	**Metrics:** Accountable for costs and number of leads	**Metrics:** Accountable for costs and revenue	**Metrics:** Accountable for ROI and forecasting revenue

Figure 2.3

THE WORD FROM SALES

So far, I've given you a glimpse of what revenue marketing means to marketers and why it is an innovation that is here to stay. But what about sales? Let's take a moment to look at how revenue marketing impacts sales.

Like marketing, sales is also undergoing a forced transformation. As I've mentioned before, prospects are typically 60–70 percent through their buying journey before a salesperson is even aware of their interest. By this time, sales may have lost the opportunity to shape the conversation. They may have ceded control to the client and lost competitive advantage, in danger of becoming a commodity. Sales is struggling to win in this new digital world and savvy sales groups are turning to marketing for help.

According to a recent study published by CSO Insights (see fig. 2.4), only 30.5 percent of all sales leads are generated by marketing. As a result, in many sales organizations today, the sales team itself is still generating some 45 percent of the leads they work! As an ex-VP of sales myself, I want to tear out my hair when I think about how inefficient this is for one of a company's most costly resources—sales. In contrast, we see elite revenue marketers contributing up to 75 percent of the pipeline from marketing activity.

2013 SALES OPTIMIZATION STUDY RESULTS
LEAD GENERATION ANALYSIS

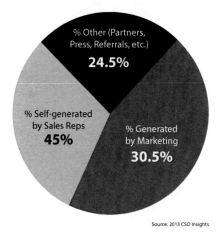

Source: 2013 CSO Insights

Figure 2.4

In the same study, sales VPs were asked to rate the services provided by marketing, including number and quality of leads. Sixty-seven percent said the number of leads did not meet expectations, and 52 percent said lead quality did not meet expectations. In general, 47 percent of sales executives thought marketing needed to improve in combined quantity and quality of leads (see fig. 2.5). If sales is the ultimate customer of marketing, this is like receiving a 4 or 5 on a Net Promoter Score where 9–10 indicates sales is "promoting" the good work of marketing, 7–8 means sales is passive about what they are getting from marketing, and 0–6 means sales is a detractor of marketing—they are not happy with either quantity or quality of leads.

2013 SALES OPTIMIZATION STUDY RESULTS QUALITY/QUANTITY OF LEADS GENERATED BY MARKETING

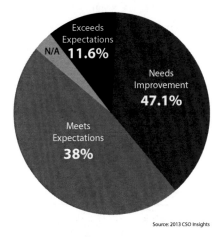

Source: 2013 CSO Insights

Figure 2.5

Ideally, marketing (a less costly resource) should be responsible for filling the top of the sales funnel with sales-ready leads, allowing sales to spend 100 percent of their time working qualified opportunities and closing business. While many marketing organizations are working on lead generation, based on this report, there is still a large gap between lead expectations and lead reality.

To underscore the need to better allocate sales time to opportunities and marketing time to the top of the funnel, look at this next statistic found in Figure 2.6. In the same study, when VPs of sales were asked what they most wanted to improve in sales effectiveness, the number one response (48.9%) was "enhancing lead-generation programs." This was the fourth year in a row VPs of sales reported this as their top initiative. The second most cited initiative was "aligning sales and marketing" (38.3%).

2013 SALES OPTIMIZATION STUDY RESULTS
SALES EFFECTIVENESS INITIATIVES

Initiative	Percentage
Enhancing Lead Generation	48.9%
Aligning Sales and Marketing	38.3%
Improving Rep Access to Key Information	36.8%
Revising Sales Process	33.4%
Enhancing Team Communications	30.4%
Analyzing Customer's Buying Process	27.2%
Revising Sales Tools	26.6%
Revising Sales Team Structure	25.3%
Revising Channel Strategy	24.5%
Revising Compensation	24.0%
New CRM Tools	21.7%
Revising Hiring Strategy	15.3%

Source: 2013 CSO Insights

Figure 2.6

Clearly, there is a need. VPs of sales have named it their number one initiative and are turning to marketers for help with revenue. Now it is up to marketers to respond and to collaborate with sales. Just ask Andrew Devlin of Brinker Capital.

Sales Collaboration

– Andrew Devlin, Communications Specialist at Brinker Capital

"Today, marketing and sales work together and collaborate on ideas for campaigns. For a while, marketing would create the content, messaging, demographic, and distribution and put it out there for sales to run with. But now, *they* are coming up with the ideas. They are on the front lines and know what our clients want most at any given time, so their input makes our marketing that much more dynamic. We have proven the value, and they understand how powerful it is."

KEY PLAYS
There are four Key Plays from this chapter. Your order may vary.

---

1. Assess where you are on the Revenue Marketing Journey:

   • Where are you, and where do you need to be?

   • How will you get there?

   • What will happen if you do *nothing*?

2. Involve your team in the assessment:

   • Ask each member of your team to read this chapter and assess where he/she thinks the marketing group is on the journey.

- Get the team together and discuss differences, decide on a position, and begin setting your course for revenue marketing.

3. Begin the Revenue Marketing dialogue with your executive team:

- Begin socializing how marketing can play a new role in revenue.

- Uncover the biggest revenue issues and socialize a new way to address them through marketing.

- Socialize marketing acting as a revenue center with ROI accountability.

4. Begin the Revenue Marketing dialogue with sales:

- How has the buyer changed, and how prepared are you to work with that change?

- Would it be useful to engage with a prospect earlier in the sales cycle?

- Would it be useful to know what prospects are interested in, and at what stage of the buying process they are in *before* you call them?

- Would you like marketing to supply you with leads that convert to opportunities at a predictable rate? What would that mean to your business?

"Most marketing executives get the concept of revenue marketing. It's operationalizing revenue marketing that keeps them up at night. But it's really not that difficult if you break it down into six key elements—strategy, people, process, technology, content, and results. We call these elements the RM6."

– Jeff Pedowitz, CEO and President of The Pedowitz Group

"Participating in the RM6 exercise was an eye-opening experience for our team. Not only did everyone get a revenue marketing view into each of our functions, but we were able to all get on the same page and put together a cohesive plan for moving forward.

– Amy Hawthorne, B2B Revenue Marketing Leader at Rackspace

"RM6 was a good point of discussion and using each of the six controls as a framework helped us clearly articulate the need for additional resources and headcount, given where we were on the journey.

– Rachel Dennis, Director of Lead Generation and Retention at Getty Images

3

OPERATIONALIZING THE REVENUE MARKETING JOURNEY

Has reality hit you yet? Marketing's role is changing, and revenue contribution from marketing will soon be—if it isn't already—an expectation from your company. Lots of marketing executives get "stars in their eyes" at the concept of a revenue marketing initiative. But the hard work is still ahead. The real question is how do you *operationalize* this strategy?

Key questions at the "stars in the eyes" stage include:

- How do I, as a marketing leader, take my company on this journey?

- How do I determine what I need to do and in what order?

- What is our best path, and how fast can we go?

- How do I operationalize this strategy into manageable projects?

- How do I transform marketing from a cost center to a revenue center?

- How do I get a seat at the revenue table?

- How do we become revenue marketers?

As we've worked with over 1,100 companies, each taking their own unique revenue marketing journey, we've helped marketing executives around the globe answer these questions, get past the stumbling blocks, and successfully transform their marketing organizations from cost centers to revenue centers. Based on this body of work, we've developed a six-control model called the RM6 (Revenue Marketing 6). This model is a simple yet strategic guide that defines *how* to transform marketing from a cost center to a revenue center.

THE RM6 MODEL—OPERATIONALIZING THE REVENUE MARKETING JOURNEY

The RM6 model leverages the key controls of Strategy, People, Process, Technology, Content, and Results. Do not read these six controls and think generically. These are elements that need to be tightly defined in terms of *revenue marketing*. Taken together, the use of these six controls creates the strategic road map for transformation.

THE PEDOWITZ GROUP
RM6 MODEL

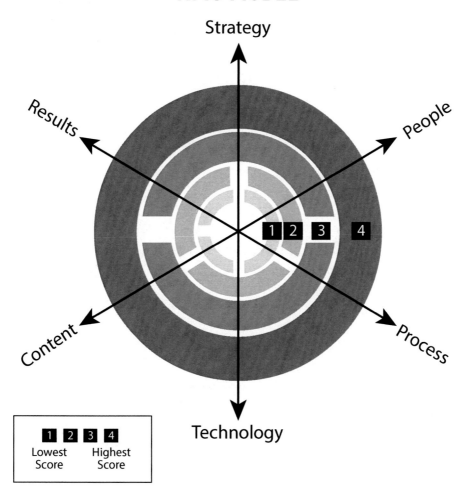

Read how Rackspace used the RM6 framework to create team cohesion and a specific revenue marketing road map.

Identify Gaps and Build a Road Map

– Amy Hawthorne, B2B Revenue Marketing Leader at Rackspace

Rackspace, a global provider of open cloud computing services, was at the demand generation phase of the revenue marketing journey and wanted to accelerate their efforts. They assembled a cross-functional team to conduct an RM6 assessment to uncover gaps and set priorities across each of the key elements (strategy, people, process, technology, content, and results).

During the one-day workshop, scoring quickly revealed that team members had varying perspectives on marketing performance across each of the six elements.

"Participating in the RM6 exercise was an eye-opening experience for our team. Not only did everyone get a revenue marketing view into each of our functions, but we were able to all get on the same page and put together a cohesive plan for moving forward," said Amy Hawthorne, B2B revenue marketing leader at Rackspace.

"In my experience, marketing teams typically don't consider all of these components when building out their revenue marketing strategy," Amy said. "We still tend to work in silos, so the team responsible for, let's say content, isn't really thinking about the other five levers of the RM6 and how this impacts content."

As a result of the team participating in the RM6 assessment, Rackspace created and executed a cohesive and agreed upon revenue marketing road map for the rest of the year.

RM6 MODEL IN PRACTICE

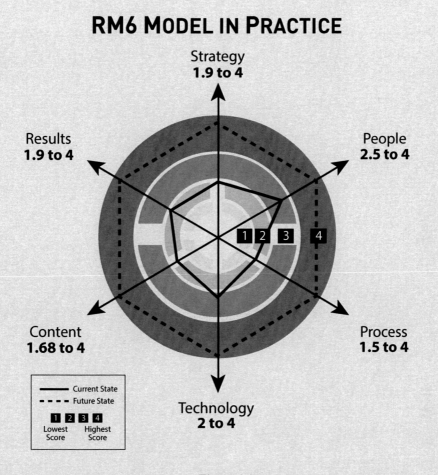

Figure 3.1

The RM6 is a qualitative assessment based on a 1–4 rating scale, with 1 being the lowest score and 4 being the highest (or best) score. The solid line on the graph represents the current state, and the dotted line on the graph represents their future or desired state in the next twelve-month period. The 1–4 ratings closely align to the four stages of the Revenue Marketing Journey so the higher your score, the closer you are to achieving Revenue Marketing. This RM6 was completed as a group exercise at Rackspace and became the road map for their revenue marketing efforts.

RM6 DETAIL

Now that you have a high level understanding of the RM6, let's examine the detail that forms each control. We'll examine each element from Figure 3.2, the RM6 model.

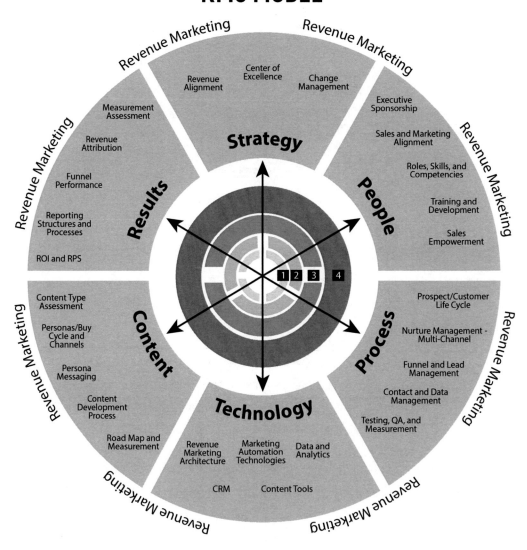

Figure 3.2

STRATEGY

Strategy is built using *all* of the journey controls and all elements within each control. This means that if you have built a revenue marketing strategy, you have a plan that encompasses all elements depicted in the RM6 model.

More specifically, there are three key elements to a revenue marking strategy that need to be discussed: Revenue Alignment, Center of Excellence, and Change Management. We have separate chapters describing the Center of Excellence (Chapter 5) and Change Management (Chapter 6).

Revenue Alignment refers to the alignment of marketing strategies and sales goals. This sounds like a reasonable requirement, yet it is stunning how many marketing organizations do not even know what the revenue number is for their company. Here is an example.

WORKING IN SILOS

I was recently working with the marketing group at a multibillion-dollar technology reseller company. I had about fifteen marketers in a room, and we were spending the day together to create a revenue marketing road map using the RM6 Assessment.

This company was at the very beginning of their journey. One of my first questions was: How are your goals aligned with the sales team's goals?

I got a lot of blank stares, and my next questions took the situation from bad to worse.

This group not only didn't know even the basic revenue number for which sales was responsible, they didn't know any of the specific sales goals, such as focus on net new business, or how to determine whether or not all deals are equal.

They didn't know any specific sales initiatives or any of the areas sales was working to improve or the sales team's current state of quota attainment.

This marketing team was working in a silo completely separate from sales. My first recommendation to this company was to get this information, fast!

Center of Excellence (CoE) refers to building a specific organizational structure that fully enables revenue marketing. The CoE moves revenue marketing from a loose coalition of roles and responsibilities to a dedicated and committed structure and set of roles.

We have dedicated an entire chapter (Chapter 5) to building a Revenue Marketing Center of Excellence. Why? Because CMOs need to put their money where their mouths are. You simply cannot transform an enterprise marketing organization from being a cost center to a revenue center without a different organizational structure, complete with new roles, skills, and compensation in place. This is an advanced level of maturity for revenue marketing.

Change Management refers to managing change along the journey. This is becoming a hot topic of conversation as marketing executives realize that revenue marketing is not only about the technology platform, but about driving and leading change around how revenue is generated in a company and the role marketing plays in this new reality.

In the interviews conducted for this book, change management or aspects of change management were mentioned by every interviewee. We have an entire chapter dedicated to the topic—Chapter 6. But what you need to know right now is that, as a marketing leader, you'll need to have a plan for change and take an instrumental role in driving this change.

I typically see marketers score themselves a 1 in this RM6 control which makes sense given when and how we engage with customers. To get to a 4 is pretty easy since this control is about whether or not you have a documented and accepted revenue marketing plan.

PEOPLE

People includes key stakeholder alignment with executives and sales and defining the roles, skills, and competencies required for a successful revenue marketing practice. This includes providing training and development for marketing and sales and empowering sales with new tools and processes.

Both Sally Lowery of Appia and Joseph Vesey of Xylem understand the importance of executive buy-in.

Executive Sponsorship

– Sally Lowery, Revenue Marketing Leader, Appia

"What's important to the C-level? Revenue. What's important for them to hear? That all of their leadership team is on board with driving that forward. Why? Because if you are serious about revenue marketing transformation, getting alignment with sales, marketing, and the executive team is the first step to selling the vision and getting executive buy-in."

Leadership Buy-In

– Joseph Vesey, Chief Marketing Officer at Xylem, Inc.

"The first thing is leadership. If you can't get leadership excited about this, then don't even start because it's probably not going to go anywhere."

One of the things to understand about this control in the RM6 is that it is not whether your people are smart and hard-working. It is more about whether they have the revenue marketing skills required. I see a lot of marketers who will score their team fairly high in this area when, in fact, they are missing many fundamental revenue marketing skills. Effective training is also a critical aspect of this control. This RM6 control also depicts the need for aligning with sales and for empowering sales with tools and processes to effectively go the last mile to revenue.

We explore "People" topics in more detail in several chapters in this book. Chapter 4 deals with the eight "starter" competencies required to begin the revenue marketing journey, and Chapter 5 introduces a more mature level of skills and roles in the Revenue Marketing Center of Excellence. Sales and marketing synergy is such an important and critical success factor for revenue marketing, we devote Chapter 7 to this topic.

PROCESS

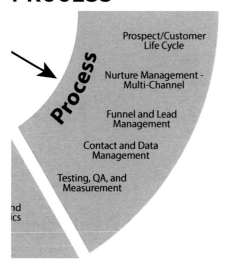

Process involves defining your current and future states and developing strategies and tactics for achieving your future state. It is the marketing executive's responsibility to set up collaboration from the top down and to ensure collaboration across all functions. I often see marketing scoring fairly low on this RM6 element, and I also see a lot of intent to map these processes and little follow-through.

The Power of Process

– Liz McClellan, VP of Field
   Marketing for PGi

"Our goal is to grow marketing-sourced revenue from 11 percent to 20 percent over the next twelve months. We're doing this with no budget increase, just by changing processes. This is a huge leap forward for us."

Many marketers just beginning their journey make a mistake by not involving sales in the beginning as they develop key processes. For example, you can't map an optimal customer life cycle without involving sales. Likewise, you can't map an optimal nurture campaign without effective lead scoring (which requires input from sales) or effectively manage a funnel without clear lead definitions developed hand in hand with sales. Successful revenue marketers not only develop and document these with sales but work with sales to continually refine and optimize these processes over time.

BUT WE DEVELOPED LEAD DEFINITIONS!

I was once working with a client reviewing their key processes, including the common lead nomenclature they had developed as part of their Life of a Lead map (what is a lead, what is an MQL, etc.).

I couldn't believe my ears when I heard one of the marketers complain, "We developed these lead definitions, gave them to sales, and they pay no attention to them!"

What's wrong with this picture?

The process control of the RM6 includes the prospect/customer life cycle, nurture management, funnel and lead management, contact and data management, and testing, QA, and measurement.

Understanding the prospect/customer life cycle helps revenue marketers understand how, when, where, and why to engage digitally with prospects and customers. Nurture management speaks to how marketing sets up long-term digital dialogues that coax a prospect through their buying journey. Funnel management is about marketing managing the marketing funnel, and lead management is about how leads flow and are acted upon between sales and marketing. Contact and data management is about data hygiene that allows effective segmentation and personalized dialogue. Finally, every marketing group needs to establish a testing, QA, and measurement process and stick to it!

As you develop all of these key revenue marketing processes, you will learn, like Amy Hawthorne at Rackspace, that communication between sales and marketing is key.

Automated Lead Management

– Amy Hawthorne, B2B Revenue Marketing Leader at Rackspace

Though the lead management process at Rackspace, the open cloud company, is still evolving, this doesn't stop marketing from keeping score.

In order to gain full insight into how things convert in both the marketing and sales funnels, marketing tracks how many leads are generated, how many marketing qualified leads (MQLs) get passed to sales, the conversion rate of MQLs to sales accepted leads (SALs), and the conversion rate from SALs to sales qualified leads (SQLs) or opportunities.

When MQLs are accepted and become SALs, the time frame in which they convert to SQLs (opportunities) is tracked to help determine the overall quality of the leads.

"If MQLs are converted to opportunities within three months, then we say that we are passing on *qualified leads*—or at least a percentage of them," said Amy Hawthorne, B2B revenue marketing leader at Rackspace.

As this new lead management process was beginning, some sales reps didn't recognize when MQLs were being passed to them. Marketing overcame this challenge through additional education and by alerting sales reps through CRM. If a rep fails to accept an MQL—or at least log it and explain *why* he is not accepting—within forty-eight hours, a notification is automatically sent to both Amy and the sales rep's manager.

"In the beginning, I was getting tons of these e-mails as there was a lot of confusion," said Amy. "Now that everybody is on the same page with our automated lead management process, I get maybe one e-mail a month. And of course, that sales rep gets a call from me."

TECHNOLOGY

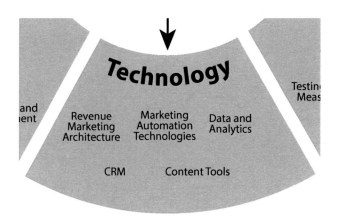

Technology is the one area that many executive marketers tend to shy away from, but revenue marketers must overcome this fear because it is critical to your success. This RM6 control includes Revenue Marketing Architecture—all of the components in your technology stack that enable all aspects of your revenue marketing transformation. This includes marketing automation, CRM, and technologies for managing content, data, and analytics. The integration of these systems (and more) is mission critical for the revenue marketer. Just ask Shawnn Smark at Bio-Rad.

Integration is What Achieves One Customer View

– Shawnn Smark, Head of Group Marketing at Bio-Rad

"Our customers don't care about our systems; they only care about their immediate experience with our company. They are interacting with many different touch points including our website, order management, e-mail, content management, and marketing automation. What we care about is having that 360-degree view of the customer so we can then provide the best value during the interaction and have a much higher chance at conversion. Having integrated systems allows us to accomplish this."

Marketing automation technologies are the big enablers of revenue marketing. Without this critical technology component, it is very difficult to achieve automated, closed-loop reporting and for marketing to directly and demonstrably impact revenue. Jim Kanir of Billtrust recognized the value of integrating these systems early in his career.

Visionary Software

– Jim Kanir, SVP of Sales and Marketing at Billtrust

Jim Kanir, a serial revenue marketer, recognized the power of digital marketing and was an early adopter of marketing automation technology.

"Today, if you haven't bought in, you can't even compete. Marketing automation went from becoming a visionary piece of software to something that is required as table stakes if you want to compete in this digital age we are in now," said Jim.

"How do you compete against a rival who is nurturing everybody and you are not? It would be like not having a website. You have to have it. You have to have the content. You have to be on point with your messaging. You have to be able to distribute that messaging, and you have to be able to get those digital fingerprints of the people who are touching that messaging and interacting with that messaging. If you don't have that, how can you possibly be successful in this landscape?"

CRM is a key ingredient to set up closed-loop reporting and revenue forecasting from marketing. Data and analytics tools allow for the cleanest database and analytics for continuous improvement, and content tools enable the development, organization, and use of content as it relates to the buyer's journey. Read how Shawnn Smark of Bio-Rad integrated CRM and marketing automation for a powerful result.

CRM and Marketing Automation—It's a Team Effort

– Shawnn Smark, Head of Group Marketing at Bio-Rad

When Bio-Rad Laboratories began its revenue marketing journey two years ago, there was no CRM program in place and, though they had something called "marketing automation," it was light on marketing and not at all automated.

"It was really a glorified e-mail service provider with no power being harnessed from a CRM system, nor did we provide for resources or workflow processes at a global or aggregated level within our product teams," said Shawnn Smark, head of group marketing at Bio-Rad.

Not only did Bio-Rad need CRM, they also needed all of the other tools required for revenue transformation. Shawnn's goal was to bring together all the marketing functions that would contribute to revenue marketing including e-business, advertising, brand building, content marketing, and customer engagement teams, and to integrate marketing automation and CRM.

"In my career, I've been around the CRM block. I've also seen the paradigm shift from multimillion dollar enterprise response e-mail packages that have to be hosted, to today's cloud-based marketing automation systems that can be hooked up to sales automation systems in a matter of days," said Shawnn. "Going in, I felt like I had a really high probability for success because, not only had the technologies matured, they're also easy to use and affordable."

Professional services had also matured, and Bio-Rad brought in seasoned people to help not only with setup, but with the organizational change needed for adopting marketing automation and revenue marketing. This helped to prove the value of the investments being made in technology and people.

As leadership began to understand the power of the technologies and transformation required to support a revenue marketing approach, they began to understand the benefits of holding marketing accountable for revenue.

Bio-Rad had everything in place in about six months and began revenue marketing campaigns on a global scale.

"The technology foundation enabled us to create an intimate experience with our customers by triggering very targeted content, which made our customers a lot happier," Shawnn said. "We now have much more reliable data, we can scale better, and we have better forecasting and planning within the funnel. Because we built a really solid foundation, we were able to see great success in about nine months."

RM6 scores for technology are typically directly related to whether or not an organization has a marketing automation system in place and for how long.

CONTENT

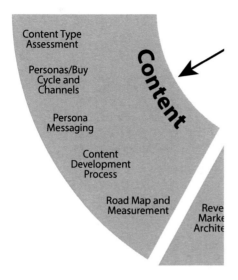

Content is the fuel for your revenue marketing journey. The foundation for a successful content program begins with using the buyer's journey and digital persona as building blocks. In the digital world, how prospects interact with your content tells you where they are on their buyers' journeys and allows you to participate in a rational and helpful dialogue. The top layer is comprised of the personas that allow you to further tailor your dialogue.

The RM6 suggests beginning with a content assessment and creating a blueprint aligned with the client's buy cycle and digital personas. Creating specific messaging for all personas, identifying a content operations structure and development process, and measuring content results are all elements of creating your unique journey.

Content is an area in which many marketers will score their organizations fairly low—even if they have a lot of content. The reason is they may have a lot of content, but it's not the right content for revenue marketing. Doug Fogwell, of AlliedBarton Security Services, and a global company I worked with share a similar content issue.

The Content Challenge

– Doug Fogwell, SVP of Marketing at AlliedBarton Security Services

"When we did our content audit at the beginning of the process, we had some 280 pieces of existing content, so I really felt we had enough and that we could just repurpose it to fit in this new environment. But when the pieces started to come together, we realized that we had a lot of content sitting in some buckets and other buckets with none and that's when it became a much bigger challenge in my mind."

I'M DROWNING IN USELESS CONTENT!

I can't tell you how many times I've heard this lament from marketers as they begin their revenue marketing journeys. Not long ago, I was working with a global company in Boston, and we were discussing the role of content in integrated revenue marketing campaigns.

The majority of the company's content was developed from the product marketing group, and they were prolific. The challenge for the revenue marketing team was that each piece of existing content was focused on a specific solution and was only useful for later in the buyer's journey. Nothing addressed a higher-level collection of solutions, and it was only useful for later in the buyer's journey.

The revenue marketing group was responsible for lead generation for enterprise companies and needed content for the earlier stages of the buyer's journey and content that presented a more holistic, value-added solution.

The marketing team was finally able to secure the budget to create the content they needed to fuel their revenue marketing practice.

RESULTS

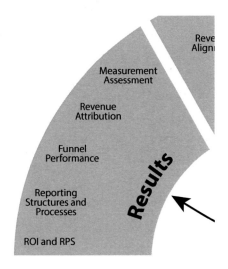

Results is the final control and also represents the ultimate measurement of revenue marketing. Revenue marketers seek delivery of ROI and the ability to forecast their impact on revenue. They work to make key metrics available twenty-four hours a day, seven days a week and want to create a marketing machine that drives repeatable, predictable, and scalable revenue impact. However you report your results, data is required. Read how Patty Foley-Reid at Iron Mountain uses data to prove her point.

Data Proves My Point

– Patty Foley-Reid, Director of Inbound and Content Marketing at Iron Mountain

"The magic happens in the sales force automation where we are tracking activity over a period of time," said Patty Foley-Reid, director of inbound and content marketing for Iron Mountain.

When a big deal comes through, Patty and her team roll up their sleeves and do the research to map out when the contact entered the system, from which program, and how long ago.

"For some big deals, marketing's influence may have started years ago when we met someone at a tradeshow and entered them into Salesforce.com from that event," said Patty. "We can see that over the past three years, for example, they have consistently gone to that event year after year. We can see that we sent an e-mail campaign to them and they engaged on three, four, five different content assets and attended our webcast. I can then paint a picture to say that maybe sales would have found that opportunity on their own and closed the deal without marketing's help, but here are the data points to show where marketing influenced that particular individual."

There are other times where marketing may have influenced an individual over a long period of time in several instances, but this particular person isn't the ultimate decision-maker. In this case, the marketing influence proof is in the data.

"We then have to analyze how many activities or touches were involved for that *account*. Ultimately, we can roll it back to say, these five people are in our system and while the fifth person is the decision-maker, he shows no marketing activity, while the other four have heavy activity over a short period of time and clearly had some influence in the buying decision."

RM6: STRATEGY TO EXECUTION (S2E)

The RM6 is a framework that speaks in executive terms. It grabs their attention, involves them in strategic dialogue, and provides a high-level set of next steps from that strategic dialogue. The RM6 also provides an easy to follow road map that moves revenue marketing from a strategy to an execution plan. For many marketers who are new to revenue marketing, this is a huge first step.

Thinking Strategically

– Dianne Conley, VP of Marketing Systems, K12 Inc.

"We now have the capability to cast a wider net to nurture folks along the way and get them to a point of readiness to interact with someone. We had to think more strategically about what was going to enable us to leverage the power of the technology because we knew that technology alone wouldn't solve our problems. We needed a coherent strategy and business process. It got to the point where we were no longer comfortable as old-school marketers. With the way technology is changing, if you're not out there reading and learning all of the time, you are going to get left behind."

KEY PLAY
There is only one Key Play from this chapter.

1. Conduct an RM6 Assessment exercise:

- Using this chapter as your foundation, have each of your team members complete the RM6 assessment (http://www.pedowitzgroup.com/RM6-Assessment).

- Review individual answers and variances in answers.

- Facilitate a discussion around answers and variances.

- Come to agreement on your number (1–4) for today and for the future.

- Decide on priorities and develop parallel work streams.

- Create one project plan with all work streams.

- Track and measure.

" Revenue Marketing is how we run marketing, and we needed people who saw the vision and believed we could accomplish this. We had to make some hard decisions at the beginning. We didn't have all the right people on board, so we had to bring in outside experience to build our revenue marketing team. "

– Liz McClellan, VP of Field Marketing for PGi

" Once we began the revenue marketing journey, we began to rearrange the skill sets on our team. "

– Chris Newton, VP Marketing, Xactly, from WRMR Revenue Marketer Radio Interview

" The specialization of your team members is instrumental to the success of your revenue marketing strategy. And by having dedicated roles focusing on each components as quickly as possible, you are ensuring that they will master it and start optimizing it much faster than if everyone is doing a little of everything. "

– Alexandre Pelletier, Independent Strategic Lead Management Consultant

4

BUILDING A REVENUE MARKETING TEAM

As a marketing executive looking to operationalize the revenue marketing journey, one of the first areas you'll focus on after making the technology decision is building out your revenue marketing team. This chapter presents the skill sets required to get up and running. In the next chapter—The Revenue Marketing Center of Excellence—we'll take these basic skills, add advanced skills, and organize them into a structure that serves a larger, more mature revenue marketing organization.

EIGHT KEY COMPETENCIES

During a recent presentation for The CMO Site on the topic of revenue marketing, I discussed the team, skills, and responsibilities required of a revenue marketing leader. I was pleased to see the high level of executive interest in the key skills that are essential to build a successful revenue marketing team.

Revenue marketing does not reside within a single role—it is a team effort—and it requires a very specific set of competencies. You may, or may not, already have some of these competencies, so read carefully.

In our experience working with hundreds of leading revenue marketing teams who have fully leveraged marketing automation tools and seen a measurable impact on revenue, we have found that the most successful organizations focus on eight specific roles and competencies to build their revenue marketing teams.

These "starter" competencies are: director or VP of revenue marketing, business analyst, power user, nurture specialist, content specialist, creative specialist, tele-qualifying team, and marketing operations. While this framework began as just five roles, it has since expanded as we gained a more intimate understanding of what is required. Further, the roles mature and change over time. This is a hot topic for executives, and I see a continued refinement and standardization of these roles in the future.

EIGHT COMPETENCIES OF A
REVENUE MARKETING TEAM

VP Revenue Marketing

Marketing Operations

Business Analyst

Tele-Qualifying - Getting Started - Power User

Creative Specialist

Nurture Specialist

Content Specialist

The Pedowitz Group 2013

VP Revenue Marketing

Role #1:
Director/VP of Revenue Marketing

The business vernacular of this role is similar to that of a director/VP of sales, as they discuss and measure the funnel, conversions, opportunities, deals, and bookings. The **director/VP of revenue marketing** is responsible for all elements of the RM6—strategy, people, process, technology, content, and results (introduced in Chapter 3). More specifically, this role is responsible for the revenue number, for building and optimizing the revenue marketing team, and for achieving buy-in and collaboration with executives and sales. This role requires strong leadership and well-tuned change management skills.

This position is generally filled by someone with a background in sales, sales operations, finance, or science. The position is often hired from outside the company rather than promoted through the ranks. Companies without this role in place typically use their marketing automation platforms as a glorified and expensive e-mail system. To successfully connect marketing to revenue using people, process, and technology, this role is an absolute requirement.

Evan Whitenight epitomizes this role. Read how Evan describes it.

I Sound Like a VP of Sales

– Evan Whitenight, Reachforce, WRMR Revenue Marketer Radio Interview

"I live, eat, and breathe in revenue-related metrics," said Evan Whitenight, director of marketing at Reachforce. "I created a dashboard for executives so we can all constantly see where the funnel lies.

"I always know where deals are—if they are getting stuck, how many deals are in the 'open' stage, where leads are in qualification status, and what is moving from inquiry to marketing qualified lead (MQL), sales accepted lead (SAL), and sales qualified lead (SQL).

"We track things like conversion percent through the stages, conversion percent to proposals delivered, close/won and close/loss analysis. I actually run these conversion meetings with sales and marketing weekly, monthly, and quarterly to discuss numbers.

"I act like a VP of sales in that I can be anywhere, anytime and I can tell you where each rep is on quota attainment, to the dollar. I am able to tell you what the pipeline looks like and where everything is by stage. I'm not as in-depth on this information as the VP of sales, but pretty close on any given day."

Business Analyst

Role #2:
Business Analyst

Revenue marketing is a new competency, and when you begin the journey, put simply, "you don't know what you don't know." As your team transitions from a creative organization to one that encompasses a focus on revenue metrics, it is the job of the **business analyst** to analyze results, set up testing protocols, and work to optimize systems and programs in order to achieve the highest and fastest revenue results.

Everything in an automated marketing campaign must be weighed, measured, and constantly reviewed. The role of the business analyst is to constantly scrutinize the numbers, because what you measure will change over time. The business analyst should be the person on your team dedicated to assessing the impact of each campaign on your bottom line.

This person is analytical, with exceptional communication skills. Because the business analyst is responsible for analyzing the numbers and reporting back to the team, both technical experience and the ability to make suggestions for change are a must. Companies without this role in place tend to be unable to reach the revenue marketing stage. Instead, they remain stuck in the early demand generation phase and are left wondering "why this stuff doesn't work."

In the world of revenue marketing, gut instinct is not good enough. Read how Liz McClellan describes this role.

Gut Instinct Is Not Good Enough

– Liz McClellan, Senior Director of Marketing, Sage, WRMR Revenue Marketer Radio Interview

"What you can't have are emotional marketers or marketers who make decisions based on gut feeling," says Liz McClellan, Senior Director of Marketing, Sage Business Solutions.

"The role of the Business Analyst (BA) is incredibly important as he reviews every single nuance from the time a prospect engages until they close. The BA needs to have deep analytical skills, is familiar with behavioral marketing, and can step back and look at data and intelligence from both an executive and sales standpoint. The BA works to optimize our activities so we can get to a revenue result quicker."

Role #3: Power User

Technology is the driver for revenue marketing, beginning with integrating your CRM system with a full-featured marketing automation system. The **power user's** role is to set up and execute campaigns, while continuously leveraging the technology to meet the needs of your business.

These marketing automation systems are powerful, and in order to get the most out of them, you must have someone on the team who is dedicated to the role and has the required technical skill set. Investing in the effective training of your power user should be a priority.

For many companies, identifying the power user is the first step. Read how Chris Newton of Xactly took this first step.

New Skills on the Team

– Chris Newton, VP Marketing, Xactly, WRMR Revenue Marketer Radio Interview

"Once we began the Revenue Marketing Journey, we began to rearrange the skill sets on our team. One of the first things we did was to find a contractor to help us run trade shows and events. This freed up a very talented individual on my team to be the power user of our marketing automation platform. She was logical, analytical, and detail oriented—all requirements of a successful power user."

The power user skill set is an absolute requirement for the team. This person will work closely with the business analyst and should be detail oriented, application friendly, and have the ability to both understand the technology and use it effectively. Experience with HTML and CRM is highly recommended.

While CRM skills abound in the market, finding marketers with marketing automation experience is a challenge. In 2012–2013, our clients took an average of four to six months to find individuals with any of these specific skills. Take your time and find the right fit. There is a high correlation between revenue results and advanced competency in marketing automation systems.

Nurture Specialist

Role #4:
Nurture Specialist

Nurture specialists are obsessed with creating an intimate digital dialogue at all phases of the buying cycle and providing qualified leads to the sales team. This role focuses on the long-term digital relationship with prospects and customers across all channels and must work with all team members to build and execute campaigns that get results.

The nurture specialist is more than a campaign manager. This role takes direction from the director/VP of revenue marketing, analytics from the business analyst, best practices from the content and creative teams, and knowledge from the power user to ultimately design the most effective campaigns.

Content Specialist

Role #5:
Content Specialist

The **content specialist** is responsible for envisioning, creating, delivering, and testing content associated with any and all parts of the digital dialogue. In other words, any content you use in any campaigns, whether inbound or outbound.

This role is strategic, tactical, and critical, as content is the currency for your ongoing discussions. A key responsibility for the content specialist is to work with a cross-functional team to build and institutionalize a Buyer's Journey Map.

This map defines the stages of the prospect's buying cycle, who participates in each of the buying stages (persona), with what type of content, and at what stage each person prefers to interact. Establishing this map enables the content specialist to work with all available resources to deliver the required content. It's important to validate your Buyer's Journey Map with a wider internal audience, as well as an external audience.

For example, in many companies just beginning the revenue marketing journey, content may be developed as a matrixed activity and involve different groups within marketing. Marketing communications may be responsible for the company messaging, website, and inbound content, while product marketing is responsible for product slicks and brochures. Until your company has a fully-enabled content function dedicated to revenue marketing, your content specialist may need to work with all of these different groups.

A TYPICAL BUYER'S JOURNEY

Awareness 〉 Interest 〉 Development 〉 Negotiation 〉 Acceptance

In order to be a successful revenue marketing organization, you need an effective content machine to feed your demand generation engine. This is a function that will grow and mature over time—and in fact, many marketers are now treating this as a full-fledged publishing function. Characteristics of this kind of approach include content that is flexible and reusable across multiple channels; content that is targeted by type, persona, and client buy cycle stages; and content that is served dynamically.

Content for Buy Cycle Stages

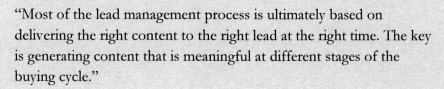

– **Alexandre Pelletier, Director of Marketing, Acquisio, WRMR Revenue Marketer Radio Interview**

"Most of the lead management process is ultimately based on delivering the right content to the right lead at the right time. The key is generating content that is meaningful at different stages of the buying cycle."

Content Manager Is Key Role

– Chris Newton, VP Marketing, Xactly, WRMR Revenue Marketer Radio Interview

"Another key role we had to find was a content manager. I mean you can put together an amazing nurturing campaign, but if you don't have anything good to send, if you don't have content that will engage people and entice them to respond, you're going to have a challenge. And this role is so much more than a writer. It's all kinds of content for revenue marketing from social media content, to well-constructed e-mails and content pieces like best practices or success tips that provide value to the digital relationship. We hired from the outside and we hired someone with a journalism background. Given the sheer volume of content we needed, plus the ability to engage the reader with good stories and points of value, she was a great fit for our team."

Creative Specialist

Role #6:
Creative Specialist

While marketing is typically considered a creative field, revenue marketing calls for an effective mix of creativity and science, and this dynamic impacts the role of the creative specialist.

In revenue marketing, the purpose of the **creative specialist** is to not only grab attention or further explain a concept, but most importantly to elicit a specific digital response, which requires a specialized creative framework. Creative can't be just about how "pretty" it is. In fact, sometimes pretty doesn't work at all. Creative for the revenue marketer is about how *effective* it is, meaning, does it help the customer or prospect engage in a digital discussion?

For example, you may find that, for a particular program, plain text e-mails will outperform those with beautiful graphics and landing pages. The point is that you need to continuously test and keep all elements of creative focused on eliciting a desired action from the digital dialogue.

The creative specialist role on your team must have a strong background in HTML, along with the ability to conceptualize how creative will be used and what "action" the campaign, landing page, or asset is ultimately trying to invite. The key to success is trying out different things to see what works. Test, test, test!

Tele-Qualifying

Role #7:
Tele-Qualifying Team

There is a trend in revenue marketing that once an MQL (Marketing Qualified Lead) has been created, it is then turned over to a tele-qualifier to follow up with a call to further qualify for BANT (Budget, Authority, Need, and Timing.) The role of the **tele-qualifying team** is critical to revenue marketing success for many companies. Such a company is AlliedBarton Security Services.

Not Just Dialing for Dollars

– Doug Fogwell, SVP of Marketing at AlliedBarton Security Services

"I have heard almost across the board from VPs of sales how impressed they are with the quality of the people we have in place. These are not your average 'dialing for dollars' telemarketers. These folks know their way around and ask very good questions. They are also impressed with not only the level of sophistication of the technology we are using, but the entire process. We're taking it to a whole new level and they recognize that."

First, this team serves to qualify an MQL for BANT prior to passing to sales. This adds an additional qualification layer beyond lead scoring and typically results in much higher acceptance rates from sales and higher conversion rates to opportunities. Second, the tele-qualifying team can provide a much needed, live "soft-touch" to prospects to ensure they are in the optimal nurture track. In addition, because telemarketers sit at a desk all day, they are in the perfect position to respond in a timely manner to "Contact Me" forms. This is important because someone completing this kind of form is ready to have a conversation and may have contacted several companies. Finally, the tele-qualifying team sits between marketing and sales and can provide immediate feedback on campaigns and work collaboratively with sales to ensure timely follow-up.

This model works best when the tele-qualifier role reports directly to marketing. When this role reports to sales, it is often called upon to take on other responsibilities, which dilutes its effectiveness. Immediate feedback to marketing is invaluable when it comes to attaining higher quality leads.

Kristen Wright at Pinstripe effectively uses a tele-marketing team.

Bringing in Tele-Services

– Kristen Wright, VP of Marketing at Pinstripe

"With the complexity of our industry and how high touch our salespeople are, bringing tele-services inside improved the handoff and maximized use of our technology. Now we actually research before calling, capture accurate notes, and put leads in the right nurture track. We use social media, e-mail, and the phone as channels, as opposed to focusing so much on just the phone."

Marketing
Operations

Role #8:
Marketing Operations

In the early 1990s, sales was transformed with the introduction of CRM technologies. As sales began to use key technologies to help run the business of sales, the sales operations position grew in many companies.

Marketing is taking a similar path with the introduction of numerous types of marketing technologies—marketing automation, web analytics, social tools, CMS tools, etc. I am seeing a marked rise in the **marketing operations** function, especially within larger companies. This is a trend that will continue and a function that is further defined in the Revenue Marketing Center of Excellence chapter.

THE TALENT CHALLENGE

Revenue marketing is still in its early stages and, as a result, finding and hiring the right skill sets for your revenue marketing team can be challenging. These competencies are highly valued and still somewhat scarce. On average, our clients take four to six months to find trained and experienced revenue marketers in all different roles.

Marketing automation tools have changed the way marketing is measured as an organization and the way marketers view themselves. Once you begin viewing your marketing organization as an asset to the business that is directly responsible for generating revenue, the next step is building an effective team that is up to this challenge.

These eight competencies will form the basic team required to get you started on your revenue marketing journey. Some companies, especially enterprise and global companies, need additional skills and structure, both for efficiency and revenue impact. This optimal level is what I call the Revenue Marketing Center of Excellence, which I'll cover in depth in the next chapter.

We're the Revenue Marketing Team

– Ken Robinson, VP of Revenue Marketing at NAVEX Global

"Across the organization, we are now recognized as the revenue marketing team, not just marketing."

KEY PLAYS

Whether you are just beginning your Revenue Marketing Journey or are in the process of optimizing it, identifying skill gaps and having a plan for how to address those gaps is crucial. There are five Key Plays from this chapter.

1. Based on the eight competencies discussed in this chapter, assess which skills you have on your team and which ones you do not:

- If you do not address the skills gaps, what will be the impact on your Revenue Marketing efforts?

2. Determine how you will get these skills, when, and with what budget:

- Train

- Hire

- Outsource

3. Determine how the new role(s) fit into your current marketing structure:

- What will change in current roles?

4. Develop a compensation structure:

- These roles are typically well compensated and are highly sought after.

5. Develop a training and education plan:

- Must be ongoing.

"Building out a Revenue Marketing Center of Excellence can take from six months to three years. It's not an overnight journey. It's not something where you can get everyone in a room, align on a strategy, and knock it out in a couple of months. This takes a lot of hard work and a lot of deep thought around people, process, and technology to support what's best for the organization as a whole and ultimately, what will provide the best customer experience."

– Nancy Harris, SVP/GM at Sage

"When we started our Revenue Marketing Journey, we started with a small team. Once we got the technology foundation in place and had some practical experience with revenue marketing, we knew it was time to reassess the global team structure supporting revenue marketing. In 2012, we began to build our Revenue Marketing Center of Excellence and are in a much better place to support the business needs."

– Rachel Dennis, Senior Director, Lead Generation & Retention, Getty Images

"A Revenue Marketing Center of Excellence is a natural progression for a company on the journey to revenue marketing. This is a mature competency. Much like the changes that CRM brought to sales and sales process, marketing automation integrated with CRM is bringing to marketing. As companies intake these technologies and fundamentally change how marketing works, we are seeing more and more companies adopt a Center of Excellence philosophy and structure."

– Bruce Culbert, Partner and Chief Service Officer, The Pedowitz Group

5

THE REVENUE MARKETING CENTER OF EXCELLENCE

Like any other strategic initiative in an organization, nothing says commitment more than a job description, a new compensation plan, and a new organizational chart. In Chapter 4, I presented the competencies to get started in revenue marketing. This chapter presents the Revenue Marketing Center of Excellence (RMCoE)—an enterprise model creating a shared services group and a corresponding field marketing structure that is designed to optimize efficiencies and effectiveness for a revenue marketing practice. The RMCoE is an advanced competency in revenue marketing and one that typically occurs over time as revenue marketing becomes institutionalized in an organization.

I will explain this organizational model, roles in the structure and definitions, and discuss how these roles work with other parts of the company.

The Revenue Marketing Center of Excellence is responsible for driving repeatable, predictable, and scalable revenue performance (RPS). In effect, a new way for an organization to grow top-line revenue—something that can't be achieved by less than a 110 percent commitment.

PROFILE OF AN RMCOE

In working with over 1,100 companies, we have found that the most successful ones—those in which marketing drives repeatable, predictable, and scalable revenue results—have an "organizational" commitment to this endeavor. Though the organizational models vary, they all share certain commonalities:

- Revenue marketing is not a disparate group working outside the main marketing group. Instead, they are fully integrated and empowered in a way that makes sense for the business.

- This group is recognized for requiring special skills, competencies, and pay structures.

- Roles are specific and well defined.

- There is a "shared services" aspect to the model to support highly specialized skills and to help improve efficiencies for larger and global companies.

- Sales and marketing are tightly aligned, both at corporate and in the field structures.

- Senior management looks at marketing as a revenue center, not as a cost center.

- Marketing reports on and forecasts contribution to revenue.

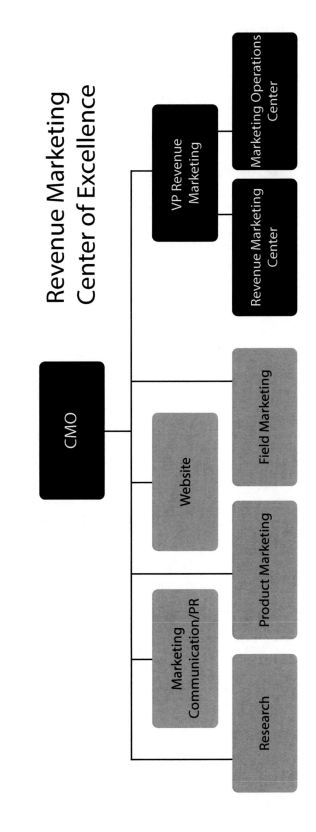

THE PEDOWITZ GROUP
REVENUE MARKETING CENTER OF EXCELLENCE

Revenue Marketing
Center of Excellence

Figure 5.1

THE RMCOE STRUCTURE AND DETAIL

Building an RMCoE can only be led by the highest level marketing executive and is a strategic initiative requiring the alignment of global sales and marketing leadership, management and team members. It crosses corporate and field business units in terms of sales priorities, pipeline, leads, reporting, and budgets.

The RMCoE is an HQ and field structure that matrixes with other parts of the organization such as the web team, MarCom, and field marketing and sales. It includes two primary sets of functions: a Revenue Marketing Center and a Marketing Operations Center (see fig. 5.1).

The Revenue Marketing Center is comprised of people skilled in creating, building, launching, and reporting on complex multichannel programs. The primary goal of this team is to first pass "sales-ready" leads to sales that close at a predictable rate for both new customer acquisition and install-base marketing, and second, to help accelerate *opportunity to close* velocity. This team is accountable for a revenue number and KPIs that support attainment of that number.

The **Marketing Operations Center** is made up of people skilled in marketing technology, Software-as-a-Service (SaaS), data management, process innovation and optimization, metrics and analysis. They provide the infrastructure, processes, and reporting that power the RMCoE.

There will be some variability in the structure of these centers and their functions. Ultimately, you have to decide what works best for your organization. But the guiding principal for determining where a team should live is based on whether they offer a service that is more infrastructural and supportive, or one that is more day-to-day, tactical-program related.

In 2012, Nancy Harris led a cross-functional team at Sage to design a Center of Excellence. Sage uses the terms "revenue management center" and "revenue performance management."

Center of Excellence

– Nancy Harris, SVP/GM at Sage

For Sage, building a revenue management center (RMC) was the best way to streamline its marketing efforts and processes and transform marketing into an organization that could grow revenue more effectively and help build a dominant master brand.

Though all of Sage's individual business units were doing great work using marketing automation and customer relationship management technology to drive revenue, there was a strong desire to consolidate efforts to share learnings and to leverage Revenue Performance Management (RPM) to its maximum potential across the company.

"We recognized the power in RPM and believed that we could communicate more effectively with our customers and prospects by speaking to them with one voice," said Nancy Harris, SVP and general manager at Sage. "We had been communicating with customers by product line and now we have the ability to be clearer and more consistent with our communications regarding the spectrum of offerings that Sage has for small- and medium-sized companies. Our goal is to make it easier for customers to determine which product best suits their needs and allow them to choose based on optimal fit."

As a first step in building the RMC, the Sage team defined the core functional roles they would need within the center and began looking for a leader of the RMC who had done this before.

The resulting RMC is a centralized group of shared marketing services consisting of a centralized demand center and marketing operations center that enables Sage to effectively communicate with its customers and prospects, build its master brand, and leverage key corporate assets and best practices.

"We took the business case to our senior management team and were able to show them how we could achieve a hard dollar return on the investment within a very short period of time," Harris said.

As one client described it when getting executive buy-in for their center, "The aspect that really intrigued them was not just the ability to centralize our messaging and build the dominant master brand, but the ability to measure everything through the funnel, understand the dynamics of the funnel, and predictably and reliably forecast based on what was going in at the top of the funnel. It drove home the point that when you couple marketing with sales this closely, you have the ability to hold both functional organizations accountable for the resulting revenue."

KEY ROLES IN THE RMCOE

The first and most important role to consider is the leader for revenue marketing. In the RMCoE structure, this is a **VP of revenue marketing,** who reports directly to the CMO, EVP of marketing, or EVP of marketing and sales.

The VP of revenue marketing is responsible for the ever-evolving impact marketing makes on revenue, best practices optimization, and building the proper alignment and ongoing collaboration among executive stakeholders in the company. If alignment at the top is not in place, revenue marketing will not work, as it requires substantive change management across the entire organization.

The **VP of revenue marketing** is responsible for:

- setting the vision and direction for the RMCoE—both the revenue marketing team and the marketing operations team;

- leading change and alignment across executive stakeholders;

- creating and executing on the Revenue Marketing Road Map;

- building relationships with key stakeholders, especially sales and channel teams;

- tightly integrating with field marketing;

- providing a quarterly and annual revenue forecast and achieving that number;

- establishing best practices, standards for generation, and optimization of marketing productivity through the use of people, process and technology; and

- proactively managing change for the ever-evolving role of marketing in revenue production.

Once a company decides to build a Revenue Marketing Center of Excellence, hiring the VP of revenue marketing is typically the next move. Once this position has been filled, it is time to create a Revenue Marketing Center and a Marketing Operations Center within your organization.

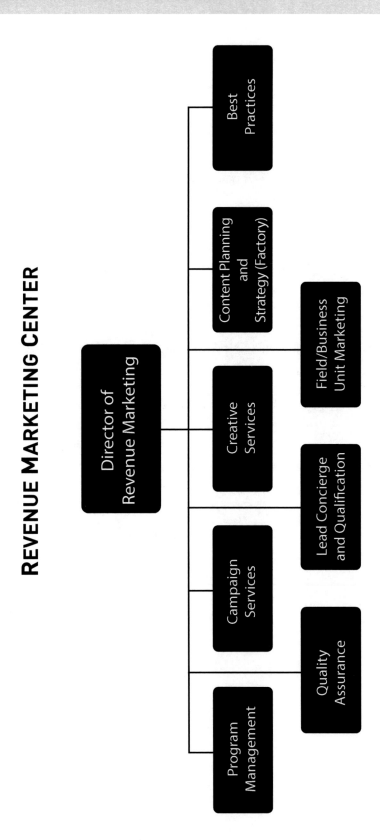

Figure 5.2

REVENUE MARKETING CENTER

The goal of the Revenue Marketing Center is to drive repeatable, predictable, and scalable revenue performance from new and existing customers through streamlined processes and optimized best practices. Figure 5.2 outlines this organizational structure.

The **director of revenue marketing** leads this group. He or she is responsible for managing the lead funnel and must be able to envision effective campaigns to your target markets. The director of revenue marketing must have a deep understanding of your market, your buyers, and how to read prospects' digital body language. They must also be results-driven and have a deep understanding of the processes that drive marketing and be able to effectively optimize the sales and marketing relationship.

The Revenue Marketing Center incorporates a number of functions that report to the director of revenue marketing, including:

1. Program management

2. Campaign services

3. Creative services

4. Content planning and strategy (factory)

5. Best practices

6. Quality assurance

7. Lead concierge and best practices

8. Field/business unit marketing

Program Management

This team envisions and executes top-down programs that align to revenue goals and ensures a revenue marketing result.

Program managers are responsible for programs across all channels—e-mail, inbound, search, social, etc. They may also be responsible for a solution set, geography, account type, or customer type (install base versus new, for example). In larger or global companies, the program manager sets up programs that can be tweaked and executed at a local or regional level.

This role takes direction from the director of revenue marketing, receives analytics from the business analyst, takes input from the content and creative teams, works closely with all of the affected stakeholder groups, and uses knowledge from the marketing automation power user to ultimately design the most effective programs.

TYPICAL ROLES/COMPETENCIES FOR THE PROGRAM MANAGER:

- Ability to envision and execute programs

- Quarterbacks programs

- Serves as business owner's point of contact for programs

- Gathers business requirements from field marketing, sales, and channels

- Establishes program business rules

- Responsible for program sign-off and authorization

- Delivers revenue through programs and proves marketing ROI

Campaign Services

The **campaign services** team consists of specialists who have the skills and expertise to operate the various technologies used to execute integrated campaigns.

Members of this team work with the program managers and may also be a shared resource across the field business units. This team sets up and executes campaigns/programs in marketing automation systems and e-mail programs. They are responsible for integrated campaign best practices—all elements of inbound and outbound—and related results. They are also expert users in all required marketing systems.

If they are asked to also take on administration of the systems and manage provisioning of new users, training, and introduction of new releases, a case can be made for moving this team to marketing operations.

TYPICAL ROLES/COMPETENCIES FOR CAMPAIGN SERVICES:

- Best practices for integrated campaign elements (inbound and outbound)
- Marketing automation power users
- Marketing resource management power users
- SEM tool users
- PPC administrators
- Content management system power users
- Social media management tool users
- Provides basic reports on campaigns
- HTML e-mail capabilities
- HTML landing page and form manipulation capabilities
- List rental, cleansing, standardization, and import/export

Creative Services

Creative services is a shared services group utilized by program managers and field marketing. Their role is to provide and manage resources for copywriting, photography and images, graphic design, web design, and artwork. Some of these resources may be sourced internally, while others may be outsourced.

This group establishes a service level agreement with the program managers and content planning team so that quality and timeliness of deliverables is maintained. They also leverage the QA group for quality control.

In some cases, work such as copy or images may flow from creative services to the campaign services team, be placed in a program, and then sent to the QA group as a whole, rather than as individual pieces earlier in the workflow.

TYPICAL ROLES /COMPETENCIES FOR CREATIVE SERVICES:

- General .NET, Java, ASP, HTML and CSS coding (excluding campaign-related landing pages and e-mail)

- Microsite design and coding

- Print design, graphic design, and drawing for revenue marketing

- Production, printing and print vendor selection, and relationship building for revenue marketing only

- Stock photo research, selection, and purchase for revenue marketing only

- Image editing

- Copywriting and editing

- Creative direction

- Creative agency selection and management for revenue marketing only

- Interactive design and animation

- Flash

- Film, video and audio editing, and production for revenue marketing

Content Factory (Planning and Strategy)

A key player on the **content team** is the content "czar." This person is responsible for a holistic content strategy that optimizes all content in the RMCoE. Since content is the fuel for the revenue marketing engine, this role is critical to revenue marketing success.

The content strategy includes what content to develop, what it will be used for, how to develop content efficiently, how to use that content piece across multiple channels, content organization, and measurement of content.

The content team plans, gathers, and organizes revenue marketing-focused content, including the website and all hard copy and digital assets. They also leverage the creative services team to create new materials.

This team has the challenge of formulating a road map for the design, creation, QA, repurpose, publication, syndication, and retirement of content specifically for revenue marketing.

They work with product marketing and marketing communications to leverage the correct messaging, positioning, and copy for campaigns, programs, and the website *as it specifically relates to revenue marketing*—not messaging in general.

TYPICAL ROLES/COMPETENCIES FOR THE CONTENT CZAR AND CONTENT TEAM:

- Creates, organizes, and manages all assets for the RMCoE

- Measures the efficacy of all content

- Serves program management with assets for campaigns

- Serves channels and sales teams with sales tools

- Directs creative services to write copy, landing pages, offers, sales tools, and websites for revenue marketing

- Determines content mix, media, distribution channel, and how to repurpose content for revenue marketing

- Responsible for (and reports on) content effectiveness for revenue marketing

- Maintains editorial calendar for revenue marketing

Best Practices

It is a requirement for every organization that seeks to learn, grow, and continuously improve its performance to centralize its earned intellectual revenue marketing capital, seek out and assimilate the wisdom from outside, and disseminate this combined wealth to the entire organization.

TYPICAL ROLES/COMPETENCIES FOR BEST PRACTICES SPECIALIST:

- Gathers, publishes, and trains on information regarding which techniques and practices yield the best results in e-mail, landing pages, forms, direct mail, data imports, reporting, dashboards, multichannel campaigns, nurturing, lead management processes, lead qualification, website design, content, and data management

- Ensures adoption of best practices by regular inspection of activities

- Oversees campaigns to ensure best practices are used

- Documents and presents findings in person and on an intranet

- Researches industry best practices in areas mentioned above

- Defines SLAs between marketing and sales and between teams inside revenue marketing

- Defines common revenue marketing language and terms

- Obsesses over prospect and customer experience

- Creates playbooks and templates for marketing activities such as campaign creation or data imports

In the event that the global field marketing team is not part of, or matrixed to, the revenue marketing team, this group may also serve as a global revenue marketing liaison.

Quality Assurance

Quality assurance is a separate team so that members can operate independently and remain objective. If their objectivity is paramount, this team could be moved into operations, but since they focus on more daily tactical tasks—such as campaigns and collateral—they are a better fit in the revenue marketing group.

This team must have the skills to accept and interpret functional requirements documents and then be able to match those requirements to the campaign, website, and collateral-related products they are given to QA.

TYPICAL ROLES/COMPETENCIES FOR QUALITY ASSURANCE:

- Creates quality reports and makes recommendations for people/process improvement

- Detects and notifies quality problems

- Inspects, reviews, and approves programs, campaigns, and documents to ensure they are flawless (includes review of HTML, target lists, selected offers, links, launch dates, boilerplates, etc.)

- Inspects, reviews, and approves processes to ensure they are optimized

- Establishes and enforces quality standards for collateral, campaigns, and processes

- If documents or campaigns must adhere to health, safety, or financial regulations, this group ensures that they are in compliance before sending to a compliance department for final sign-off.

- Educates marketing departments regarding specific quality requirements

- Ensures a flawless customer experience

Lead Concierge and Qualification

It is becoming more common to find a **lead qualification** group in marketing. This group is recognized by various names, such as telemarketing, tele-qualifying, lead development, inside sales representatives, etc.

In some cases, where they are encouraged to sell lower priced services and products, they belong more in sales than in marketing. But in cases where their role is to simply cultivate prospects, qualifying them before passing the lead on to sales, it is more valuable to keep them in marketing. This further connects the revenue marketing team to their ultimate deliverable to sales and to the channel, which is warm, qualified leads and an accelerated funnel.

For this team to be successful, it is critical to set up a defined and documented lead management process with clear lead quality rules, hand-offs, and service level agreements. Measuring the number of calls they make per hour, for example, is not an important exercise in measuring results. The real measure of results is the number and percentage of Sales Accepted Leads (SALs) they generate per month.

The goals of this group should be based on net SALs, which are qualified leads passed to sales minus leads rejected by sales. Many companies also measure the number and dollar amount of opportunities created from MQLs.

TYPICAL ROLES AND COMPETENCIES FOR LEAD CONCIERGE:

- Participates in multichannel campaigns that require human interaction

- Live person/live chat support (sales, not support-related)

- Prospect concierge service to assist buyers in the buying cycle with no sales pressure

- Elicits BANT (budget, authority, need, and timeline) criteria from leads in the funnel

- Elicits prospect characteristics to narrow them to a specific persona (for better marketing)t

Field/Business Unit Marketing

Field marketing is typically structured by business unit or geography. In the new RMCoE model, this group may also be matrixed into the Center of Excellence as it relates to revenue marketing activities.

TYPICAL ROLES/COMPETENCIES FOR FIELD/BUSINESS UNIT MARKETING:

- Gathers customer requirements for the business unit/geography to be sent back to the revenue marketing team—specifically the program manager

- Localizes marketing messaging and collateral to better fit the business unit's needs

- Builds and maintains relationships with local sales (direct and channel)

- Revenue marketing in the region for local direct sales and channel partners

It is typically beneficial for field marketing to be connected, at a matrix level, to the center of excellence team. By connecting field marketing to this organization, they will be able to more easily:

- influence the content and offers that are produced;

- copy marketing campaigns that are launched in other regions;

- consume, create, and share best practices;

- leverage the centralized creative services group;

- leverage the centralized QA group;

- leverage the campaign services group to configure business unit level campaigns;

- leverage the reporting and analytics group; and

- add their voices to that of the RM Center of Excellence to lobby for change within the technology group, data management group, process optimization group, and the reporting and analytics group.

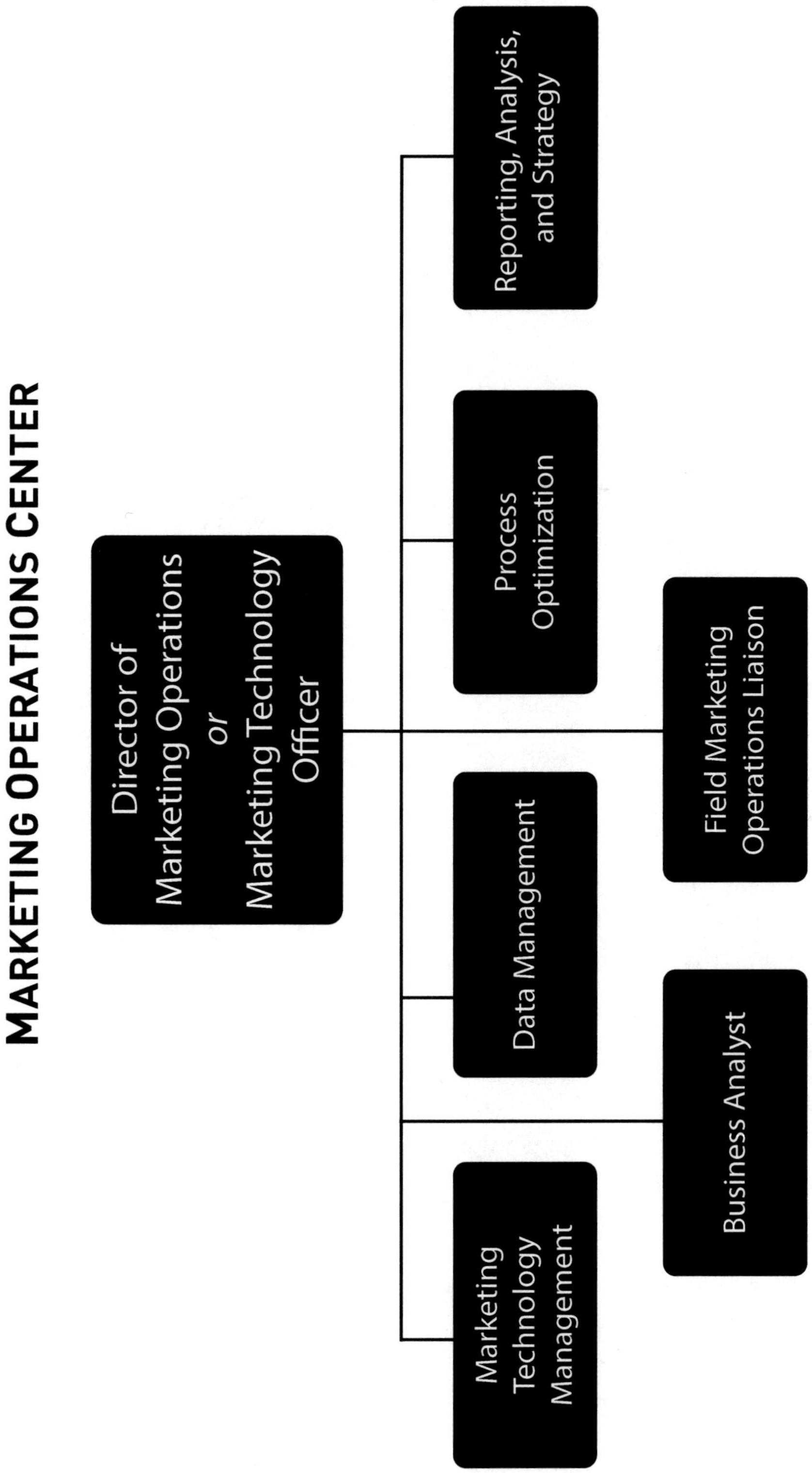

MARKETING OPERATIONS CENTER

Figure 5.3

Director of Marketing Operations *or* **Marketing Technology Officer**

- Reporting, Analysis, and Strategy
- Process Optimization
- Data Management
- Field Marketing Operations Liaison
- Business Analyst
- Marketing Technology Management

MARKETING OPERATIONS CENTER

The goal of the **Marketing Operations Center** is to optimize marketing effectiveness with leading edge technology, optimized processes, clean and current data, and rigorous analysis and reporting (see fig. 5.3).

When I originally began writing about the marketing operations group, I defined the leader as the director of marketing operations. Since then, based on rapid changes in the market, I've added a new role to this group—the marketing technology officer (MTO).

RISE OF THE MTO

Today's marketers are using technology—specifically marketing automation platforms—to make dramatic impacts on revenue.

In a recent study from Lenskold Group and The Pedowitz Group, 68% of the 373 marketers surveyed are using some type of marketing automation system. While this is interesting and certainly shows growth in this space, what is even more interesting is the business result from using this kind of technology. It's a fact: marketing automation integrated with CRM helps companies outgrow their competition.

Companies using marketing automation with CRM reported greater growth than their competition 66% of the time, while companies without marketing automation reported greater growth only 50% of the time.

This kind of data is fueling the use of technology in marketing to the point where marketing needs to proactively embrace technology as a key competency in their organization—not outsource it to the IT department. The time for the marketing technology officer is now.

A recent report from Gartner tells us that marketing automation will be the fastest growing category in CRM over the next four years and that by 2017, chief marketing officers (CMOs) will have a bigger IT budget than chief information officers (CIOs).[1] This should be a real wake-up call for any B2B

---

[1] "A Marketing Software Convergence on the Horizon," Chuck Schaeffer, CRM Search, http://www.crmsearch.com/marketing-automation-social-marketing.php.

marketing group that has delayed jumping into the marketing automation and social marketing fray. The message is clear: if you want to remain competitive, you'll need to master these technologies.

Another recent article on CMO.com discussed the proposition from Forrester that companies need to hire a marketing technology officer to manage all customer facing technologies.[2] I love this article, as it works well within the center of excellence framework and really emphasizes the need to effectively use and manage technology as a game changer for marketing.

For today's CMO, the question is, "How do you begin to understand all of the technologies you'll need in order to survive and thrive?"

1. Start with a high-level review of the various technologies that are being used in companies similar to yours.

2. Talk to other CMOs and heads of marketing about how they are addressing the optimization of technology.

3. Get your team involved in the assessment of various technologies. You'll probably find them more ready than you can imagine.

4. Try something! Pilot technology in a specific area of your business. This will help you learn while gaining alignment and buy-in on the value of the technology.

5. Finally, depending on your business needs, decide if an MTO should be on your radar.

In absence of an MTO, the **director of marketing operations** leads the marketing operations group. In larger, multinational corporations, this function will have a centralized group that leads and controls all group operations with people in locations around the world that have a significant marketing presence.

---

[2] "Forrester: Sell the idea of a marketing technology office to CIOs," Derek du Preez, *Computerworld UK*, last modified November 07, 2012, http://www.cmo.com/articles/2012/11/7/forrester-sell-the-idea-of-a-marketing-technology-office-to-cios.frame.html.

The Marketing Operations Center incorporates a number of functions, including:

1. Marketing technology management

2. Data management

3. Process optimization

4. Reporting, analysis, and strategy

5. Business analyst

6. Field marketing operations liaison

Marketing Technology Management Group

This group is intimate with the business needs of revenue marketing and uses this knowledge to provide technology and services to marketing to make them more productive. They leverage resources in IT, outside agencies, and vendors for implementation of most solutions.

The reason this group exists outside of IT is because they need to be close to the business requirements and must marry the work of agencies with their internal marketing teams.

TYPICAL ROLES/COMPETENCIES FOR MARKETING TECHNOLOGY MANAGEMENT GROUP:

- Defines the business requirements for marketing technology and service providers

- Selects and engages new agency and vendor resources, including SaaS providers

- Creates and maintains a revenue marketing technology road map and oversees release management with contingency planning and risk assessment

- Interfaces with IT, vendors, sales ops, and the CRM team

- Governs systems including SLAs, QoS, security, administration, and problem resolution, as well as related technology and service training and adoption

- Likely to also be a CRM administrator, perhaps as a backup to the sales operations CRM administrator

- Serves as an administrator for all applications rolled out for marketing, including MRM, MA, CMS, PPC, databases, business intelligence tools, e-commerce tools, website hosting services, and collaboration tools

- Responsible for any customization that these products or services may require

- Oversees data integration between disparate marketing systems and other data repositories

Data Management

If the data master is the CRM system and marketing automation syncs to this system, it is probable that the ownership of the data—and therefore much of this role—resides in sales operations. In the event that this role does not exist (and there is an opportunity to add it into the marketing operations group), this is a general description of what is needed.

Data quality can decline in many ways. Data naturally loses accuracy over time (decay), it becomes corrupted (loss of integrity), duplicates can be created (loss of cleanliness), and new data can be added that is simply incorrect (loss of accuracy and lack of completeness).

If marketing invests $100 for each new lead, for example, then a 100,000 record database is an asset worth $10 million. Without proper data management, this asset will depreciate at 2 percent per month. (In just two years, half of the records will be invalid!) Because of this, the success of your marketing campaigns is absolutely dependent on the quality of your data.

TYPICAL ROLES/COMPETENCIES FOR THE DATA MANAGEMENT TEAM:

- Maintains data quality through rigorous data analysis, standards definitions and adherence, data hygiene (contact management, health of customer database, etc.)

- Creates and runs reports to identify quality issues and remedies

- Responsible for all data integrations including field mapping, data flows, and CRM

- Oversees data segmentation (list management)

- Drives data quality rules, procedures, new processes, and the standards for normalization of data entered into the system

- Manages reporting on data quality metrics

- Trains on best practices in entering new data

If the role of data steward exists in sales operations, marketing will still need to check that their requirements are met to ensure campaign success. This includes the assurance that first and last names of all leads and contacts are accurate; lead and contact owner information is up to date; segmentation data is correct; dynamic content and targeted lists are accurate; customers, prospects, employers, partners, vendors, investors, media, and competitors are clearly differentiated; and all contact dates and lead statuses are up to date and accurate.

Process Optimization

This group is responsible for ensuring that the processes that control and direct marketing activities are optimized for both efficiency and productivity. This team may also be a place to include certified project managers who could direct large marketing initiatives, marketing technology releases, etc.

TYPICAL ROLES/COMPETENCIES OF PROCESS OPTIMIZATION:

- Innovates new marketing processes and redefines old ones

- Measures the efficacy of current processes

- Oversees project management for major marketing initiatives

- Changes management function

- Creates and maintains processes training and documentation, including lead management (lead flow); integrations between marketing automation and CRM, MRM, and CMS; processes and workflows around asset creation and website updates; CAN-SPAM and related regulations; new marketing technology and services rollouts; and SLAs and the integration of sales processes with marketing processes.

Reporting, Analysis, And Strategy

This vital group is responsible for the in-depth reporting on revenue marketing activities and attribution to revenue. This is a good place to centralize all of the revenue marketing analytics and business analysis. As a result, this group is often best positioned to help on budgets and to provide data for planning efforts.

TYPICAL ROLES/COMPETENCIES OF THE REPORTING, ANALYSIS, AND STRATEGY GROUP:

- Oversees web and campaign analytics

- Compiles historical results, current activity measurements, and results projection including dashboards, funnel reporting and analysis, interpretations and recommendations based on results, suggestions for A/B testing methods to hone results, and weekly/monthly/quarterly annual reports to multiple levels of management

- Measures marketing ROI, reporting, and accountability

- Links investments to revenue projections to guide decision-making

- Analyzes marketing automation/CRM data

- Uses business intelligence systems

- Participates in company initiatives where deep data and analytical knowledge is required

Business Analyst

Everything in an automated marketing program must be weighed, measured, and constantly reviewed. The role of a **business analyst** is to constantly analyze the numbers, because what you measure will change over time.

The business analyst should be the person on your team dedicated to assessing the impact of each program on your bottom line. This person should be analytical and possess exceptional communication skills. Because the business analyst is responsible for analyzing the numbers and reporting back to the team, both technical experience and the ability to effectively make suggestions for change are a must.

The business analyst could live as a separate group or be part of the reporting group or campaign management group.

Field Marketing Operations Liaison

This group or individual is the link between marketing operations at the Center of Excellence and the many field offices. The **field marketing operations liaison** will assist with global technology/service rollouts and adoption; global process change rollouts and soliciting input from field marketing; managing global data issues—particularly when certain locations are experiencing accelerated data decay; and managing the unique field marketing requirements for reporting.

This person or group is the CoE-based voice of the field marketing team. They are advocates for the needs of the field marketers and responsible for communicating back to those field teams what they need to know to be prepared for upcoming changes.

DIVISION OF LABOR

When a company moves to develop a Revenue Marketing Center of Excellence, some consolidation and re-arranging of responsibilities typically occurs. One question I am often asked is, *what is the responsibility of the CoE versus the field?*

Center of Excellence vs. Field

Does the entire revenue marketing team need to be located together under one roof? Which functions can be in the field versus at the RMCoE?

Our general recommendations are shown in the chart below, but this can vary depending on your business environment. The third column—Outsource with RM Agency—means that early in the development of your RMCoE, an expert revenue marketing agency can help you accelerate time to competency and can work as a natural extension of your team until you are ready to do this on your own.

CENTER OF EXCELLENCE ROLES:
CORPORATE, FIELD, OUTSOURCED

	Best at Corporate	Best In the Field	Outsource with a Revenue Marketing Agency
Program Management	✓		✓
Campaign Services	✓		✓
Content Planning and Strategy	✓		✓
Creative Services	✓		✓
Quality Assurance	✓		✓
Lead Concierge	✓	✓	
Field Marketing		✓	
Best Practices	✓		✓
Marketing Technology Management Group	✓		✓
Data Management	✓		✓
Process Optimization	✓		✓
Reporting, Analysis, and Strategy	✓		✓
Field Marketing Operations Liaison	✓		

INSOURCING VS. OUTSOURCING

Quickly hiring, training, and integrating a revenue marketing team into your marketing organization can be a challenge. For this reason, you may want to consider outsourcing some parts of the revenue marketing team until other members of the team have mastered their roles.

110

Outsourcing some revenue marketing functions allows you to:

- Quickly find, assemble, and deploy skilled marketing people to revenue marketing tasks.

- Lower the risk of poor technology adoption by bringing in skilled users.

- Easily align and integrate the efforts of sales and marketing by using people who already know how to do this.

- Quickly obtain the desired ROI on technology, data, and process investments.

- Acquire best practices knowledge transfer from industry leading experts faster.

- Avoid the pitfalls that naturally occur in the revenue marketing journey.

Developing a RMCoE typically occurs once a marketing group has some experience and a better understanding of how revenue marketing can impact their organization. This is an advanced competency. Rachel Dennis of Getty Images discusses how they grew into this structure.

Maturing into a Revenue Marketing Center of Excellence

– Rachel Dennis, Director of Lead Generation and Retention at Getty Images

Getty Images, a leading content provider, conducted a business process review which forced the company to look at sales and marketing alignment, including structure, best practices, funnel development, and management and reporting.

Rachel Dennis, Director of Lead Generation and Retention at Getty Images, was assigned to kick-start the process. She immediately started selling the vision and benefits of revenue marketing to obtain executive buy-in and secure the resources required to implement a marketing automation solution and build a revenue marketing team.

As she talked about the power of an integrated sales and marketing funnel and described the ability to show revenue impact from marketing campaigns—along with having insight into where to invest in marketing campaigns and the impact down the funnel on sales revenue—sales became more interested.

Rachel began to identify the key roles required and started to slowly build a revenue marketing team. She knew they needed to start with the technology foundation and then build skills and resources from there. As Getty Images' revenue marketing maturity grew, the global team also expanded, and soon it was time to support the initiative with a more intensive structure.

In 2012, Getty Images began to build their Revenue Marketing Center of Excellence.

Their RMCoE includes four groups: Campaign Services, Campaign Strategy, Creative Services, and Analytics and Reporting. A particular focus for Getty Images was Campaign Services, and they needed an experienced leader for this area.

"We hired an individual who came in with the experience and attitude that was exactly what we needed to drive us along the road map at a much, much faster rate," said Rachel. "This person was really the catalyst to move everything forward."

The *Campaign Services* group consists of five people, split between New York and London, who handle e-mail programs for both internal and external projects and serve as custodians of best practices and testing strategy. As the power users of the technology, they set up, test, and deploy campaigns around the globe and ensure that program objectives are met.

The *Campaign Strategy* group is made up of program managers responsible for strategy and development of customer life stage programs. They leverage the services and expertise of the campaign services group to ensure that all program objectives are being met.

"The Campaign Strategy group really owns the business issue, solution, identification and, ultimately, the success of our nurture programs, as well as our newsletter strategy and direct outbound calling programs," said Rachel. "We are recruiting now for a second full-time manager and a full-time executive for this group, with two people based in New York and one in London."

Creative Services, based in New York, reports to the Senior Campaign Services Manager and is responsible for the design and copy writing for our campaign assets, including e-mails, landing pages, forms, and newsletters.

Analytics and Reporting, based in Seattle, provides reporting analysis and insights to support business and program decisions within the team, as well as for external stakeholders.

"They also play a marketing operations role working directly in CRM," said Rachel. "And for direct lead sources—those leads that do not go through any lead nurture program, but go directly to sales—they are responsible for maintaining those sources and changing any of the associated sales assignment logic."

An RMCoE model is a new idea for marketing and may require a substantial investment, but that investment should be aligned to an equally significant return. You will want to take the time to carefully calculate investment/return on an RMCoE as part of your presentation to senior management to ultimately fund this transformative initiative.

Early Adopter

– Lawrence DiCapua, Leader of GE's Revenue Marketing Center of Excellence

"Companies should look at revenue marketing as an evolving discipline and get in early to become a part of the evolution of this new field. It's an opportunity to really make a difference in your business before it becomes traditional practice."

KEY PLAYS

This entire chapter is a Playbook for how to build and organize a Revenue Marketing Center of Excellence. So, instead of Key Plays, here are a few characteristics we see that are common in companies who have begun this initiative. Assess yourself and determine your state of readiness.

1. Massive appetite for change across the organization based on some type of disruption in the business.

2. Executive belief and advocacy for Revenue Marketing.

3. Marketing executive to lead the initiative and drive change.

4. Extensive 3–5 year business plan and budget supporting the initiative.

" I'm passionate about bringing change to marketing here, and that means changing the mindset of marketers to revenue marketers. "

– Amy Hawthorne, B2B Revenue Marketing Leader at Rackspace

" With any new concept, any change, it requires a disruption. You have to get in front of the right people, win them over, and make sure everyone is on the same team and looking in the same direction. But once you are able to get traction and prove the value, at that point you are positioned for true, scalable success. "

– Lawrence DiCapua, Leader of GE's Revenue Marketing Center of Excellence

" We had been doing the same marketing and getting the same results for the past ten years, so there was certainly some pent-up demand to change the way we did things to get more intimate with the customer, produce better results, and hold marketing more accountable. Our marketing staff was definitely at the point where they realized we were never going to scale beyond what we were unless we did something fundamentally different. There are people who invest in marketing a specific way and will never change, but I think the times will change them. "

– Shawnn Smark, Head of Group Marketing at Bio-Rad

6

REVENUE MARKETING CHANGE MANAGEMENT

Once you begin the revenue marketing journey, you have begun a transformation process, a process of change. Based on our work in helping marketing executives manage this change, we have created a model for the five stages of revenue marketing change: Disruption, Resistance, Acceptance, Adoption, and Advocacy.

THE PEDOWITZ GROUP
STAGES OF REVENUE MARKETING CHANGE

Disruption ⟩ Resistance ⟩ Acceptance ⟩ Adoption ⟩ Advocacy

This is a model that I had in mind as I recently attended two national conferences. Each had a dedicated executive-level track for enterprise companies sharing their revenue marketing stories. As I sat in the audience and listened to these case studies from top marketing executives, I began tracking how many times each speaker used the word "change"—and it was a lot. I didn't hear them talking about lead scoring or describing their most recent campaign. No, the executive level dialogue for revenue marketing was firmly centered around how this is a change and what they need to do to lead that change. What I observed during these two conferences is consistent with every discussion I have with marketing leadership who is effectively adopting revenue marketing. They see it as strategic—as a change initiative they must lead—and they understand it takes time and dedication from the top. These leaders also recognized that revenue marketing is a team effort. Cleve Bellar at Sage also believes in the power of the team.

Change is a Collective Initiative

– Cleve Bellar, VP, Marketing – Revenue Performance Center, Sage

"The biggest thing I have learned is that there is nothing worse than marching to the water and you turn around and there is no one there with you. You can't ever forget about the change element. Revenue marketing cannot be driven by individual heroes. It must be an organizational strategy and a collective initiative. As one Forrester analyst said, 'Don't let perfect get in the way of being better; just do something.'"

STAGES OF REVENUE MARKETING CHANGE

Disruption 〉 Resistance 〉 Acceptance 〉 Adoption 〉 Advocacy

Stage 1: Disruption

Disruption occurs when the marketing status quo is failing. Some tipping point has occurred, typically as a result of company performance, changing market dynamics, competition, new strategies, or shareholder influence. One of the things I have observed around disruption is the more disruption or the stronger the disruption in a company, the faster the revenue marketing journey occurs. Conversely, I've also observed that companies without significant disruption tend to move much slower.

During this early stage, there may be many obstacles, including:

- Executives who do not see how marketing can play a significant role in revenue. This happens most often in larger and more traditional organizations that are driven by sales. The company is constricted in their views due to complex and siloed organizational structures and/or older executives with no experience in marketing beyond the traditional aspects.

- The VP of sales sees marketing as the "event" and "make it pretty" department. Since sales and marketing alignment is such a critical success factor for revenue marketing, being unable to change the perspective of the chief sales officer can almost guarantee failure or a long, hard battle.

- The current marketing team is uncomfortable talking about revenue or having any responsibility in this area. "This is not what I was hired to do" is what we hear and what many marketers are thinking. This happens in companies of all sizes and is often a surprise to the executive leading the change.

In order to overcome these barriers, first assess your organization's readiness for revenue marketing. Is the marketing status quo failing? What tangible evidence do you have? What kind of business disruption is your company experiencing? Can you attach to this disruption and make it better? Prepare a valid and compelling business case for revenue marketing based on how you can help address the disruption.

- Present a new way to grow top-line revenue, save money, become more efficient and more competitive, and increase market share.

- Gather and present research. Include facts and statistics about results/success achieved by industry peers, as well as competitors. This is often a great kick-start for executives.

- Assess and recommend technology options as one of the key enablers for change. As you begin a technology assessment for marketing automation, the vendors in the space do a great job of providing you with evidence and proof of the impact these systems can make on revenue.

Business disruption (market dynamics, new technology, change in buyer behavior, etc.) often leads to a real appetite for change. Read how Kristen Wright took advantage of this appetite to introduce revenue marketing as an initiative.

Appetite for Change

– Kristen Wright, VP of Marketing at Pinstripe

When Kristen Wright joined Pinstripe, things started moving fast.

The company's leadership team wanted marketing to take a more active role in lead generation, and they had a huge appetite for change. The funnel was shrinking, and there was a sense of urgency to identify additional sources of lead opportunities for the business to keep growing.

"We had a significant advantage in terms of being able to move quickly because of the fast growth rate of the company, the high expectations of the internal stakeholders, and the performance-driven culture. We had the leeway to just move and recommend what was current and what was coming next, which for me was revenue marketing," said Kristen, Pinstripe's VP of marketing.

Historically, the team at Pinstripe had been focused on brand building, thought leadership, and event marketing—all still very relevant channels—but they didn't have a good way to accelerate and fill the pipeline on the sales side of the organization. The first step was to redesign the company's website with optimization and conversions in mind, and then choose and implement a marketing automation solution that would provide the backbone for revenue marketing.

"We've been successful very quickly," said Kristen. "Not only have we met our revenue goals for both of our key divisions, we have actually exceeded expectations for one of them."

STAGES OF REVENUE MARKETING CHANGE

Disruption ▸ **Resistance** ▸ Acceptance ▸ Adoption ▸ Advocacy

Stage 2: Resistance

I can guarantee that you will experience resistance as you begin your revenue marketing journey. Get prepared. The trick to overcoming resistance is helping stakeholders understand what's in it for them, repeatedly and in different formats. This education builds a willingness or openness to evaluate options. Here are some of the common barriers I see at this stage:

- There is no clear vision or consensus across the organization about why changes are coming and how these changes will impact everyone. If your revenue marketing initiative or optimization plans are tied to disruption, you need to create a vision for revenue marketing with the "why" and the "how" and then tie it to the larger disruptive factor in the company. This vision has to be communicated thoroughly and often.

- Marketing is not typically viewed as a "change agent." This can be a significant barrier and in this case, being a successful change agent works best if major disruption is occurring in the company. During periods of change, senior management is much more likely to look at unexpected sources for new ideas and thinking outside the box.

- Marketing doesn't really talk to sales, or the relationship between sales and marketing is not good. This is a big problem, and we hear it repeatedly from companies of all sizes.

- Marketing doesn't have a good understanding of technology and is not comfortable or knowledgeable when talking to IT. This is an area in your immediate control, so jump on the bandwagon and get yourself educated!

Sometimes resistance comes from unexpected places, like your own marketing team. Read this perspective from Fiona Nolan at CommScope.

Team Resistance

– Fiona Nolan, SVP of Global Marketing for CommScope

"Some of the earliest resistance—and it wasn't vocalized, but I could see it in people's eyes—was from my own team. You could see all of their minds were working, but this was so different. You could see the field team thinking, *This is really going to impact what I do.* I think they saw some loss of control, but as they get into it, they're seeing the opposite. It was important to manage change and to set expectations carefully."

The key to successfully eradicating resistance is to be able to clearly articulate the value proposition for each stakeholder in their terms, and to express it multiple times, and in different formats. Here are a few ideas learned from my experience—all based on communication and education:

- Identify each stakeholder group—who will be affected by revenue marketing, and how?

- Create a full-scale communication and collaboration plan. This will help you secure buy-in by facilitating a dialogue, establishing and communicating the resulting value of revenue marketing for each stakeholder group, and by getting input early in the process.

- Provide relevant education for each stakeholder group.

- Educate executives through briefings on how "aligned" sales and marketing organizations are driving revenue and outperforming the competition.

- Distribute revenue marketing case studies that clearly illustrate marketing's contribution to revenue in other organizations.

- Inform key stakeholders with your current and future ability to show ROI and revenue contribution. Present a series of "imagine this" scenarios.

- Bring in third-party expertise to help overcome resistance. It's amazing how many times we walk into an organization and repeat the same thing that marketing has been advocating, but because we are consultants, the executives and stakeholders hear it from us and begin to embrace the change. If you're stuck, use a third party who has lots of experiences and stories to share.

Stakeholder Understanding Is Critical

– Kristen Wright, VP of Marketing at Pinstripe

"It's critical from the very beginning to really understand what the stakeholders' level of understanding is about all of this. They have to know what the channels are, as well as be crystal clear on the various roles, responsibilities, and implications. Knowing where your partners are is really important so you know what kind of communication to do on the front end to sell the idea, and then what kind of ongoing communication you need to do to make it stick."

STAGES OF REVENUE MARKETING CHANGE

Disruption ❯ Resistance ❯ **Acceptance** ❯ Adoption ❯ Advocacy

Stage 3: Acceptance

Revenue marketing gains momentum during the Acceptance stage as a clear plan of action is developed. The revenue marketing plan defines why change is needed, what will change, how and when it will change, what will be the impact on all stakeholders, and who is responsible. This is the point at which having an operational plan that has been co-developed with the involvement of all key stakeholders works to gain widespread acceptance.

As with the other stages of change, there will be obstacles at this stage as well. The most common ones I see are:

- Failure to include all stakeholders with a vested interest in the outcome. Too often, marketing wants to create something "by themselves" and then roll it out to other stakeholders. This might happen because of distrust, embarrassment, avoidance, or lack of understanding for how to build collaboration.

- Failure to consider the culture when formulating the course of action. Like any change initiative, understanding and incorporating the culture of the organization can be the difference between success and failure.

- Lack of clarity around expectations and desired results. This speaks to having the aforementioned operational plan in place. You can't expect people to change without a clear understanding of the ramifications and benefits.

Like many of the stages of change, acceptance depends on the quality and quantity of communication. Here are a few successful strategies I've seen:

- Be inclusive, rather than exclusive, when it comes to formulating a revenue marketing plan. The most successful revenue marketing organizations involve all key stakeholders from the beginning. They use this input to help shape, pilot, and optimize all elements of revenue marketing.

- Clearly outline *how* you are going to achieve your new business objectives. Outline key strategic objectives of the change, tie each key process or task to the broader objective, and assign accountability. Again, this speaks to having an operational plan in place and having it well communicated.

- Develop a clear organizational chart with roles and responsibilities. This scares a lot of executives in the early stages when they see that significant change may need to occur in their team. At the same time, if you don't take this step early, you may have a marketing team filled with fear, uncertainty, and doubt. Start by building on what you already have in place and make changes as you progress.

- Provide a plan to educate and implement new skills for those who will be affected by the change.

- Foster collaboration by creating a centralized repository for all key documents that contains information about the strategy, structure, and transformation. Grant access broadly and allow team members to contribute feedback and ideas. Keep in mind that push will be more effective than pull at this juncture. Create communication campaigns that keep all key stakeholders up to date and track their interest.

- Create a PR plan to celebrate innovative ideas, key milestones, and next steps. Foster engagement by celebrating successes and highlighting milestones reached.

Remember: Acceptance evolves into adoption when strategy turns into action.

STAGES OF REVENUE MARKETING CHANGE

Disruption ⟩ Resistance ⟩ Acceptance ⟩ Adoption ⟩ Advocacy

Stage 4: Adoption

In the Adoption stage, stakeholders move from "going through the motions" to personally realizing the value of the change. This is the point at which marketers begin to refer to themselves as "revenue marketers," and synergy begins building among all key stakeholders as they embrace and optimize revenue marketing. While this is an exciting stage, there are still some common barriers or pitfalls:

- Not living up to expectations quickly enough. This is an example of being a victim of your own success. The revenue marketing journey is not easy. It has many moving parts and takes time—like any major transformation. Often, we see that sales is fully on board with the initiative and expects "the magic" quicker than marketing can actually deliver.

- Lack of clear revenue goals, roles, and responsibilities. This has more to do with adoption by the marketing team than by external stakeholders. Everything is on course at this stage, but if the senior marketing executive does not have a clear plan for goals, roles, and compensation aligned to revenue marketing, the initiative may stall—and stall quickly.

- It's also important to advertise early wins during the adoption phase. Seeing success among their peers helps drive adoption quickly and deeply.

Celebrate Early Wins

– Joseph Vesey, Chief Marketing Officer at Xylem, Inc.

"We have tried to create change at the highest level by building excitement in the business and by acknowledging early wins so that everyone is on board and willing to change systems and structures. We keep score along the way and celebrate and that helps us move very quickly."

Here are some effective strategies we have seen applied in the adoption stage:

- Build a thoughtful, detailed, and visible operational plan, with timelines that are longer than you think it will actually take. This is not sandbagging; it is accepting that you don't know all the answers because, most likely, this is your first revenue marketing journey. Communicate updates methodically—both the good and bad.

- Create and establish concrete goals, roles, and any compensation changes you need for your team and make sure they are attainable. Nothing is worse at this point than a confused and unmotivated marketing team. It's your job to set them up for success! Depending on the level of maturity you have obtained at this stage, it might be time to implement a Revenue Marketing Center of Excellence (RMCoE). This is a shared services model that optimizes efficiencies and revenue potential through a specific organizational structure and set of roles. I introduced the RMCoE in Chapter 5.

Adoption is also about recognizing the reality of change. One client we work with applies an agile software development process to help them on the journey to revenue marketing.

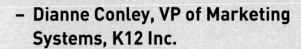

Agile Processes

– Dianne Conley, VP of Marketing Systems, K12 Inc.

"As we look to improve best practices and processes across functional teams in our organization, we apply agile processes. This means that we don't expect perfection but instead work in the reality of change."

Another key element in achieving adoption of revenue marketing is changing the mindset of the organization and of marketers. Amy Hawthorne of Rackspace discusses this aspect of adoption.

A New Mindset

– Amy Hawthorne, B2B Revenue Marketing Leader at Rackspace

"I'm passionate about bringing change to marketing here, and that means changing the mindset of marketers to revenue marketers," said Amy Hawthorne, B2B revenue marketing leader at Rackspace, a global provider of open cloud computing services.

Amy saw in her own organization—and across the board with marketers in general—that the marketing mentality is mostly focused on production and activity, not on end results.

"Just look at the average marketing organization and you'll see that they are drowning in day-to-day activities. And this is reinforced because they are measured based on number of activities completed," Amy said.

When Amy first came to Rackspace, she needed to help change the focus of marketing from activities to results. Through education and goal alignment, Amy has successfully changed the mindset to one of revenue marketing.

"Change is hard and without a driving force and structure, you simply are not going to change people's methods. Maybe that's why there aren't many revenue marketers out there yet. We have to ask ourselves, why are we doing all of this? Does it really matter? I don't think a lot of marketers know."

STAGES OF REVENUE MARKETING CHANGE

Disruption 〉 Resistance 〉 Acceptance 〉 Adoption 〉 **Advocacy**

Stage 5: Advocacy

Advocacy is born when revenue marketing becomes the *new* status quo. Marketing has a defined role on the revenue team, and the company has a new way to drive, measure, and forecast top-line revenue growth.

While revenue marketing nirvana has been achieved at this stage, there are still a few things to watch for:

- Don't be fooled into thinking that you have arrived, and the engine will just keep going without any additional tuning. Advocacy requires benchmarking, institutionalization, communication, and training on established best practices. Any key process in a company, from sales to service, needs additional tweaking and fine-tuning as tools and market conditions change.

Ways to overcome the obstacles to advocacy:

- Create a Revenue Marketing Center of Excellence or at least a Best Practices Center. Seek out and assimilate wisdom from outside, centralize earned intellectual revenue marketing capital, and disseminate this combined wealth to the entire organization.

- Create or provide opportunities to showcase your journey and shared successes at tradeshows, vendor-sponsored speaking engagements, award submissions, or leading industry events. Benchmark and publish growth and improvements.

- Give back to other marketers by sharing your story outside of the company. Benchmark your results with other industry leaders. Identify opportunities to make improvements.

- Clearly define and provide career opportunities, rewards, and recognition for revenue marketers.

- Keep challenging the status quo!

- Create an environment of innovation. The market is still immature in its revenue marketing competency, and I foresee change continuing at a rapid pace. Let the champions carry the flag. Establish a policy that gives team members the authority to make improvements to processes and metrics. Set up an awards system for revenue marketing innovation. We work with several companies who have established revenue marketing innovation awards.

It is important to remember that revenue marketing is transformational, and for it to work, you as a marketing executive must include smart change management as part of your operational plan. Change management is critical to accelerate and optimize your revenue marketing journey.

This is a big effort that requires everyone's buy-in. It is up to you to sell the vision and get everyone on your team moving in the right direction and towards the same goal.

KEY PLAY

This chapter is a Playbook on how to lead change around a revenue marketing initiative. Here is one Key Play to help you get started. I recommend you write this out, not just think it through.

1. Do a quick run-through of the Change Model to assess where you are and how ready you are for change:

- Do you have disruption? How significant? Can you attach to it?

- Where do you think the most resistance will be, and how can you overcome it?

- How will you gain acceptance? What can you use that is already in place and what will you do differently?

- How will adoption take place? Can you think of something else the company has adopted? How did this happen?

- How will advocacy happen in your company? What will it look like? How will you showcase successes?

"The thing that I find most important in all of this is sales and marketing alignment. It doesn't matter what we do on the marketing side—if sales isn't bought in and fully integrated with us, it doesn't work. It's just a marketing engine then, not a revenue marketing engine."

– Amy Hawthorne, B2B Revenue Marketing Leader at Rackspace

"It is so scientific now (revenue marketing) that if we don't do it right, we feel like we've let each other down. There's no finger pointing, but we work together to figure out where improvements need to be made. This is a total transformation from years past."

– Liz McClellan, VP Field Marketing, PGi

"Part of the challenge with alignment may be vocabulary. The phrase 'Sales and Marketing' implies separate missions and functions. Today, the alignment must be seamless and inter-operable since many roles are dynamic and symbiotic across the entire revenue generation team.

– Jim Kanir, VP of Sales and Marketing, Billtrust

7

MARKETING AND SALES SYNERGY

Revenue marketing will not happen without sales alignment—period. Across all the companies we've worked with and most recently from all the interviews I conducted for this book, alignment with sales continues to be the strongest, most persistent, and most stressed condition for success. Further, marketing leadership takes responsibility for this alignment and makes it a top priority.

"Sales alignment" is the term most often used to describe this pivotal relationship, but if you closely examine it in the environment of successful revenue marketing, a more appropriate term is "synergy." Let's look at the definition of each term and then more fully examine this critical relationship for all revenue marketers.

- **Alignment**: 1. Linear or orderly arrangement, 2. Positioning of something for proper performance, 3. Support or alliance.

- **Synergy**: Synergy comes from the Greek word *synergia*, meaning joint work and cooperative action. 1. Synergy is when the result is greater than the sum of the parts. Synergy is created when things work in concert together to create an outcome that is in some way of more value than the total of what the individual inputs are.

Which definition sounds more like a model for relationship success and for revenue marketing success? Of course, it's synergy! Synergy is the end-state description of your relationship with sales, so let's further explore what this relationship looks like.

WHAT IS A SYNERGISTIC RELATIONSHIP?

So, what does synergy look like? More specifically, what are the *behaviors we can observe* that characterize a synergistic marketing and sales relationship? Here are five characteristics I see in successful revenue marketing organizations. As you read them, ask yourself if this describes your relationship with sales.

1. Both marketing and sales use a common revenue language.

2. Both marketing and sales are vested in each other's success.

3. Both marketing and sales are proactive in their relationship.

4. Both marketing and sales work together as one revenue team towards achieving shared, revenue-oriented goals.

5. Both marketing and sales have goals and compensation tied to shared revenue metrics.

In this chapter we will look at a model for how to create a synergistic relationship with sales (the Marketing and Sales Synergy Model, see fig. 7.2). Inherent in this model is the need for change management, so to further our understanding of marketing and sales synergy, we will spend the second half of the chapter tying this all together with the Revenue Marketing Change Management model from Chapter 6.

RELATIONSHIP WITH SALES

The character of your relationship with sales correlates to where you are on the revenue marketing journey, as represented in Figure 7.1. As I walk you through the progression of the relationship, ask yourself where you are and where you need to be. There is no good or bad. There is just a beginning point in time and an understanding of where you need to be and why.

SALES RELATIONSHIP ON THE REVENUE MARKETING JOURNEY

Two, Disparate Processes	Linear Processes	Aligned Processes	Synergistic Processes
• Marketing and sales managed in silos - "Sales who?" • The MarCom Group • Focused on brand building and impressions • No B2B lead generation	• Little alignment with sales - "Hey, here's a lead." • E-mail • Tactical • One-off e-mails focused on generating leads • Focused on the cost of lead acquisition	• Aligned with sales on goals and compensation - "Here is what we agreed on." • Marketing automation + CRM • Language of Revenue • Nurture/MQLs/SALs/SQLs/Opportunities	• "Wow, look at what we did together!" • Sales and marketing are THE revenue team • Repeatable, Predictable, Scalable (RPS) processes • Mirror organizations • Systems optimized
Metrics: Accountable for costs and activity	**Metrics:** Accountable for costs and activity	**Metrics:** Accountable for costs and revenue	**Metrics:** Accountable for forecasting revenue and ROI

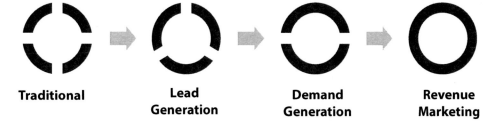

Traditional	Lead Generation	Demand Generation	Revenue Marketing

Figure 7.1

THE MARKETING AND SALES SYNERGY MODEL

We now know what a synergistic relationship looks like, and we've used the revenue marketing journey as a model for you to assess your current state—and future relationship—with sales. Let's now look at *how* to create a synergistic relationship with sales. This Playbook is a simple model we have developed based on our interactions with over 1,100 marketing and sales groups.

THE PEDOWITZ GROUP
MARKETING AND SALES SYNERGY MODEL

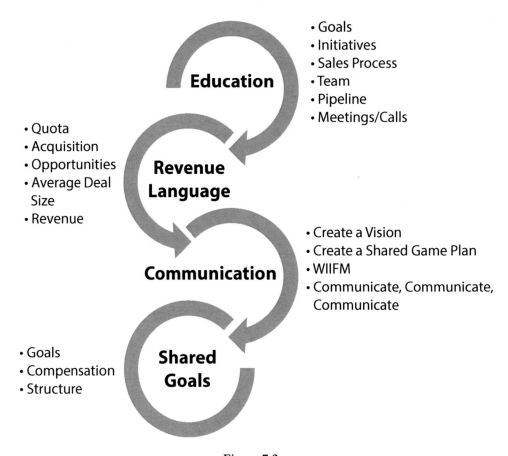

Figure 7.2

EDUCATION

The first step in creating any relationship with sales is to educate yourself and your team on all things related to sales. Trying to create a relationship with sales without understanding their world simply does not work. More specifically, you need to understand the sales *goals*, be a part of sales *initiatives*, understand the *sales process*, know the *sales team*, and educate yourself on the *pipeline*. The only real way to do this is to meet with sales, join sales meetings, and go on calls with them. If you haven't done any of these activities before, you might be surprised how receptive sales may be to your participation.

Take a step back and honestly assess yourself and your team on your current level of sales understanding and insight. If it is not where it needs to be, make this your top priority.

While you are educating yourself in the world of sales, you are also educating sales into a new world of possibilities of a relationship with marketing. A common characteristic of successful revenue marketers is that they take this journey *with* sales…from the very beginning.

Read how this happened at Pinstripe and PGi.

Beginning the Journey Together

– Kristen Wright, VP Marketing, Pinstripe

While the leadership team at Pinstripe was 100 percent on board with revenue marketing, sales buy-in was critical to really make it work. Marketing included sales early in the process, beginning with the selection of a marketing automation system.

"Two of our key industry verticals were represented on our SME team to evaluate options—not only from a program or solutions standpoint, but also from a technology standpoint," said Kristen Wright, Pinstripe's VP of marketing. "These sales VPs were involved at the ground floor, viewing demos and understanding not only what it could do for us in marketing, but also for them in sales."

Sales remained involved throughout the entire process—helping to prioritize the various industry verticals and target audiences, cleaning up the database, reviewing and providing input on content, and even designing the lead scoring model.

"We had sales buy-in from the start because they helped create the model for Pinstripe," said Kristen. "Along with accountability, we gave them a forum to provide feedback throughout, which would not only make them better at their jobs, but would enable us to deliver more qualified leads at the right time."

Tour of Duty

– Liz McClellan, VP of Field Marketing for PGi

"Marketing and sales don't sit on opposite sides of the room during workshops anymore, and meetings feel incomplete until both are in the room together. Marketing now sits in on every sales leadership call and is an integral part of the team.

In addition, we implemented a Tour of Duty as part of marketing's goals. Every marketer has to be in the field, on sales calls, and listening to what customers and reps are saying. We need to understand where we can really make a difference, and we can't be successful at this unless we're in the field."

REVENUE LANGUAGE

Revenue Language

Like sales, revenue marketers must begin embracing the language of revenue. Typical revenue marketers don't talk to sales about pretty fonts or newsletters; they talk to sales about *opportunity pipeline*, *quota*, and *revenue*. They ask sales questions like, "What number do you need to hit for your new acquisition target? What does your current opportunity pipeline look like, and how can we help? What is your average deal size, and how can we help grow that? Where are you opportunities not closing, and how can we help?"

Sales Gaps

– Sally Lowery, Senior Director of Marketing for Appia

"Marketing often has a tendency to fall short of understanding the actual sales cycle from what a prospect looks like all the way through to close. Understanding the sales cycle is critical because it helps you build your strategy and see where the gaps are in your marketing programs."

In a revenue marketing organization, you'll also observe that sales, marketing, and the executive team all use the same revenue language. They share a grounded understanding of revenue terms and use these terms consistently, specifically, and deliberately. If the CEO is listening to a quarterly update from marketing and sales, she understands the meaning of terms such as marketing qualified lead (MQL), sales accepted lead (SAL), and sales qualified lead (SQL). The CEO also understands the language of funnel conversion for marketing, as well as for sales. And, when marketing claims a direct contribution to pipeline of 43 percent, the CEO and VP of sales understand and accept the validity of this number.

Are you educated about sales, and are you involved in meetings? Are you beginning to embrace a revenue language? If not, go out and talk to sales, learn their language, and then work together to create a common language—the language of revenue marketing!

COMMUNICATION

Communication

As a leader, to be ready for revenue marketing and to engage in a relationship, you need an effective vision and a game plan. It is up to you to set the vision, create and communicate the game plan, collaborate on the game plan, and get buy-in to the game plan.

As a revenue marketer, you are a change agent. Actively engaging with sales, having a vision, and having a game plan all demonstrate your commitment, understanding, and leadership for this transformation. It also helps gain the collaboration you'll need by clearly articulating the "What's in it for me?" for each key stakeholder group.

Creating and gaining commitment to a jointly-developed game plan takes time and repetition. You can't just walk into a meeting and expect sales to "get it" in a thirty-minute presentation. After all, you've probably spent months attending conferences, reading white papers, and educating yourself about the benefits of revenue marketing. You'll need to plan for multiple communication methods, meetings, and events to share your vision and craft the ultimate game plan.

Here are a few ideas I've seen work well to develop and communicate your plan:

- Involve sales and executives from the very beginning of your journey.

- Build a persona for each role for which you need buy-in and put together a mini campaign using e-mail, face-to-face meetings, and pre-scheduled meetings.

- Set up more informal face-to-face meetings with key decision-makers and influencers to share what you know and to get their advice on shaping this initiative.

- Set up "Revenue Marketing Briefs" in pre-scheduled meetings:

    o during the weekly, monthly, and quarterly sales meetings, provide education and updates. Share the value of revenue marketing by distributing case studies from other companies. Make sure you get all views represented—marketing, sales, and executives;

- o during regularly-scheduled senior management team meetings; and

- o during regularly-scheduled company meetings.

Not everyone or every organization is as ready as NAVEX Global to embark on the Revenue Marketing Journey.

My Playbook Earned Support

– Ken Robinson, VP of Revenue Marketing at NAVEX Global

"I came in with a playbook and presented a vision with the people, process, programs, and technology to drive results. I explained the way things should be and how we were going to get there. I think it was sort of a breath of fresh air for the sales leadership—no one had talked to them this way before! But they supported me because people said, *Ken can deliver on these promises. He's got a vision, he knows where he is going, he knows how to get there, and he will deliver results along the way.*"

SHARED GOALS

I can't emphasize strongly enough the importance of sales and marketing having shared goals, aligned compensation, and complementary organizational structures. In the world of sales, no revenue accountability for marketing means *zero* respect from sales. When we take a look at the most successful revenue marketing machines, we see that marketing has the same kinds of goals as sales. If sales has a number tied to new account acquisition, so does marketing. If sales has a number for enterprise accounts, so does marketing. If sales has a number for a new product, so does marketing.

Marketing needs to have revenue marketing *accountability*, meaning that, just like sales, they are tied to and incented on a number. This is a huge change for marketing that has been fully driven by the change in technologies and buyer behaviors. When revenue misalignment occurs, it can be both costly and demoralizing. Read about how this can happen.

A REVENUE MISALIGNMENT STORY

It's 2010 and I am in New York City meeting with the sales and marketing teams of a global services company. Marketing at this company is changing rapidly and needs to be accountable for revenue. They want to be a revenue marketing organization, and they are taking the first steps on their journey.

We're running a two-day workshop designed to map the lead management process, identify roles and responsibilities across sales and marketing in that process, clarify how automation can be used, and establish a common lead nomenclature.

Prior to the workshop, we conducted twenty-six interviews with field sales and marketing team members around the world. During these interviews, we identified the first broken process: misalignment of revenue goals.

Sales, we discovered, was spending the majority of its time on existing customers because this was the easiest place to generate revenue and meet quota. Marketing, on the other hand, was focused on generating leads with non-customers, a much harder and longer sales cycle. Sourcing net new leads was also a much more costly endeavor for marketing in terms of time and resources. So marketing was sending to sales leads that they did not want to follow-up on. As a result, salespeople focused their time working the customer base and largely ignored leads for new business.

Once this discrepancy was identified, the company's marketing team changed its focus. It moved customer renewals away from the sales team and encouraged online renewals instead. This allowed sales to still earn a commission while giving them more time to work new business leads being generated from marketing.

The point is this: If marketing and sales are not on the same page around revenue goals, the cost to the organization can be quite high. If marketing is to play a key role in revenue, it requires a synergistic alignment around revenue goals, and that alignment has to begin and be advocated across senior management to have a chance at success. Finally, nothing drives home a behavior change like aligning both goals and compensation structures. Read how this happens on Jim Kanir's team at Billtrust.

Marketing is Bonused on the Sale

– Jim Kanir, SVP of Sales and Marketing at Billtrust

"About 78 percent of all sales have our marketing touch all over them, and our marketing team is actually paid bonus on Sales Accepted Leads (SALs). When a lead converts from a Marketing Qualified Lead (MQL) to a Sales Qualified Lead (SQL), we are only halfway there. We don't get anything for that. But when a salesperson takes that SQL and converts it to an opportunity, our marketing team is bonused on that sale. So, sales is actually controlling part of the paycheck for marketing. It was marketing who came up with this compensation plan. And marketing actually drives when it is time to hire more salespeople, based on the number of qualified leads."

As you begin the revenue marketing journey, it may not be realistic to have shared goals based on numbers, but you can start by aligning your activities more specifically to support sales initiatives.

Another common attribute of marketing and sales synergy is organizational structures that align or mirror one another. Patty Foley-Reid, from Iron Mountain, provides an excellent example.

Marketing Mirrors Sales... Goals, Structure, and Compensation

– Patty Foley-Reid, Director of Inbound and Content Marketing at Iron Mountain

"A big part of reaching the revenue marketing goal lies in the close relationship between sales and marketing. Our two organizations work together continually to ensure marketing's activities are directly aligned to sales efforts," said Patty Foley-Reid, director of inbound and content marketing at Iron Mountain.

Marketing mirrors the sales organization's every move. If sales reorganizes to focus on a specific product or vertical, marketing will reflect that change. If a business group has a quota with a specific service, marketing supports that effort by promoting the service that is the highest priority.

"We align ourselves with the way sales is structured to make sure we focus on shared goals," Patty said.

This includes marketing compensation to ensure that their efforts are directly tied to the sales quota. If sales gets paid more on Service A than Service B, for example, then marketing has an incentive bonus based on those same goals.

"We call it *mix matters*," said Patty. "We can hit our number and overachieve on quota, but we haven't done our job unless the product revenue mix is right. For instance, if sales has an 80 percent goal for Product A, then 80 percent of our marketing revenue should come from Product A."

The approach is working. Marketing has earned variable bonuses since the program began.

HOW ALIGNED ARE YOU WITH YOUR ORGANIZATION'S REVENUE GOALS?

Take a quick mini-assessment. How would you answer the following questions?

- Is your company looking for top-line revenue growth? If so, by how much?

- How will your company ensure this growth, and what is the role of marketing?

- Does marketing participate in the annual revenue discussion? How? As a wallflower or a vibrant and respected contributor to the revenue discussion?

- For what percentage of growth will marketing be responsible?

- Is your company looking for revenue growth from a solution area? A region? National accounts? The install base? Cross-selling? Renewals? New accounts? Hiring new salespeople?

How did you do? If you have trouble answering these questions about your organization's marketing strategies and sales goals, you are not as aligned with revenue as you should be!

APPLYING CHANGE MANAGEMENT TO CREATE MARKETING AND SALES SYNERGY

Creating a synergistic relationship with sales takes time and effort but results in a big payoff. The marketing and sales synergy model will provide the high-level guidance you need. Once you are ready to fully tackle creating that long-term synergistic relationship with sales, you will become a catalyst of change in your company.

Recognizing the role of change management (in a revenue marketing context) to improve the sales and marketing relationship will help you expedite the process. Using our change management model from Chapter 6, let's look at how to most effectively optimize your relationship with sales.

Change Step #1: Sales Disruption

STAGES OF REVENUE MARKETING CHANGE

Disruption › Resistance › Acceptance › Adoption › Advocacy

In my experience working with marketing organizations, I find that building a relationship with sales will be much faster and easier if there is some type of disruption affecting sales and/or the company. If that disruption is not there, change may still come, but it will be at a slower pace and feel like you are swimming through peanut butter. The first thing you need to do is to find that disruption around sales (this may require some digging) and attach to it.

FIND AND ATTACH

I was recently working with a company whose sales numbers were great. The VP of marketing wanted to begin the transformation to revenue marketing, but everyone seemed content with the job sales was doing, and there was no obvious disruption or driver for change. In other words, senior leadership did not see a compelling reason to change.

I sat down and had a conversation with the VP of sales. It turns out that 25 percent of the reps were driving 80 percent of the quota. In the meantime, a large number of salespeople were turning over and not meeting quota, resulting in a huge cost to the company. Here was the disruption—a problem that needed solving and one that could be addressed by revenue marketing.

My recommendation to marketing was to create a business case for revenue marketing that specifically addressed getting new reps to quota quicker and having a better chance at quota success by executing specific campaigns by reps to help build their pipeline. The VP of sales loved it, and they ultimately adopted this strategy. This became some of the first campaigns run by marketing as they executed their revenue marketing strategy.

The lesson learned is that sales disruption may not always be obvious to marketing, so taking the time to fully understand what is going on in sales can have a big payoff. In addition, sales may have an issue that they have no idea you can help them solve. Because revenue marketing is an initiative that can help you improve revenue, find out what is going on in the sales organization. Is everyone meeting quota? What is your competition doing? Are they eating you for lunch? What has changed in the market conditions? And finally, talk about the shareholders and what expectations they have. Are you meeting these expectations?

If you are going to be an effective leader and agent of change, you must participate in the revenue conversation at the executive level and show them a new way to solve age-old revenue challenges.

Change Step #2: Sales Resistance

STAGES OF REVENUE MARKETING CHANGE

Disruption ▶ Resistance ▶ Acceptance ▶ Adoption ▶ Advocacy

As with any major change, some people are going to say "no!" This will happen with some or all of your sales team—I promise! But resistance from sales is something for which you can actually plan.

What Salespeople Want

– Jeff Ramminger, Senior Vice President of Field Marketing & Client Consulting at TechTarget

"As an industry, we're still not doing the complete job of delivering intelligence to salespeople in ways that they are comfortable interacting with it and using it. For marketers to be successful, I believe in my heart that they are going to have to sell the salespeople on the value of prospect intelligence. They are going to have to come up with solutions that are cool and usable enough that the salespeople look at them and think, *Where have you been all my life? This is exactly what I needed.*"

It all comes down to knowing your audience. Confer with the sales team. Communicate with them and get them involved. Talk to them about what's in it for them. Then, write it down. Be able to show them how you can change their lives, what it will look like, and what they will get out of it. This is how Jim Kanir, SVP of sales and marketing at Billtrust, worked with his sales team to help them get on board with marketing playing a role in revenue and sales making changes in how they were selling.

Find Your Champions

– Jim Kanir, SVP of Sales and Marketing at Billtrust

As SVP of sales and marketing at leading outsourced billing services provider Billtrust, Jim Kanir remembers what he used to think about marketing when he was a sales rep.

"I thought that all of this marketing stuff was literally a bunch of mumbo-jumbo, and I was a sales guy and a gunslinger and was going to roll into town and do it my way," he said. "I think this is still the mentality of too many salespeople today. We act and behave like fighter jocks and think that, because we fly the planes, we are the most important people in the universe. There is a tendency for sales to ignore all of the support and logistics that go into making that plane fly."

When Jim came to Billtrust, it was apparent that the company had phenomenal customer references. However, as he began talking to customers, he realized that marketing was not capitalizing on this success.

"We just weren't speaking the customer's language in our collateral and on our website. So, my first objective wasn't to hire ten more sales guys, it was to fix all of our outbound content and messaging so that it was clear, crisp, and compelling," said Jim. "As we did that, we needed to get a reference point on how customers were interacting with that content."

Enter marketing automation technology. As a former sales rep himself, Jim knew how important it was to get buy-in from sales. Very early in the process, he began talking about marketing automation at sales meetings, describing what the technology could do for sales, and how it could ultimately be used to generate better, higher-quality leads.

Jim singled out two of the top salespeople and asked for their help. "I asked them what they would want to send a customer if they knew he/she was six months out from buying," Jim said. "We took their feedback and built some campaigns around what they shared. We made it less about marketing and more about sales."

The sales reps began using the system and entering prospects into nurturing campaigns. Before long, deals started coming in. In one instance, when asked if the new campaigns helped the sale, the rep responded, "Yes! This probably shaved three months off my sales cycle."

Jim asked the reps to share their success stories with peers at an upcoming sales meeting. "Instead of marketing taking the credit, we let them talk and evangelize it. As soon as the other salespeople heard the stories, they all wanted to be a part of it and set up their own nurture programs."

Change Step #3: Sales Acceptance

STAGES OF REVENUE MARKETING CHANGE

Disruption > Resistance > **Acceptance** > Adoption > Advocacy

Acceptance begins to occur when you as a marketing leader begin to operationalize your plan with sales. Though sales will likely still be cautious, they are more willing to try some new things at this stage of the process if you have fully painted the vision for how this will "rock their world!" Having those sales champions engaged *early* helps expedite acceptance throughout the sales team.

This is a great time to start working with sales on activities like mapping out the life of a lead, defining roles and responsibilities at each stage, how long a lead stays in a stage, metrics per stage, if and how any technology is used in the stage, and finally, how that lead flows from one stage to the next.

This is exactly what Liz McClellan at PGi did to gain acceptance with sales.

Gaining Acceptance from Sales

– Liz McClellan, VP of Field Marketing for PGi

Marketing wasn't always aligned with sales at Premiere Global Services (PGi), but today, it's transformed into a relationship that is more than just about alignment—it's about a strong bond built between the two teams.

"We started talking to sales about helping with revenue and how we can improve lead quality," said Liz McClellan, VP of field marketing for PGi. "We explained how we were going to move the needle together, as a team, working towards common goals. Marketing has revenue goals and will be compensated for performance against leads and revenue generated."

To kick it off, sales and marketing leaders attended a two-day workshop and came up with sixteen agreements on the lead management process. They hammered out what a lead looks like, who should get it and when, how sales will work it, and the results they expect to show.

Today, these are called service level agreements (SLAs) and are an integral part of the sales and marketing infrastructure. Sales and marketing meet monthly to talk about results and how to tweak and improve the process.

"It is so scientific now that if we don't do it right, we feel like we've let each other down," said Liz. "There's no finger pointing, but we work together to figure out where improvements need to be made. This is a total transformation from years past."

Letting sales know what's in it for them is a great way to gain acceptance. Hint: For many salespeople, this equates to meeting revenue targets.

Show Sales the Benefit

– Amy Hawthorne, B2B Revenue Marketing Leader at Rackspace

"Salespeople are very numbers oriented. They want to know the benefit to them before they invest in something, so we have to start by showing them what they will get out of it."

Remember, at this stage of the process—as in every stage—it is very important not to overpromise and then under-deliver. Transformation does not happen overnight, and this is a stage where you should be very cautious.

Change Step #4: Sales Adoption

STAGES OF REVENUE MARKETING CHANGE

Disruption 〉 Resistance 〉 Acceptance 〉 **Adoption** 〉 Advocacy

At this stage, sales and marketing are "playing nice," and things are starting to work. There are about 1,001 tactics you can use to gain adoption at this stage of the journey. For example, focus on campaigns that quickly and directly impact individual salespeople, sales teams, territories, and solutions. Do you have specific campaigns that can help salespeople who are chasing a certain quota? Do you have campaigns that will help those reps who are elephant hunting? What about campaigns to help a sales rep build a specific territory? When new salespeople come on board, are there campaigns in place to help them get started so that they are not just sitting at their desks in front of an open telephone book or browsing through LinkedIn looking for names to call?

While all of these tactics are important, focus on a higher-level approach for gaining sales adoption by executing your plan in bite-sized chunks focused on producing quick wins for sales. This was a common theme found across many of the interviews conducted for this book, and the larger the company, the better this approach works. Rather than trying to "boil the ocean" and be all things to all people, you need to narrow your focus to a series of highly prioritized and visible projects you can control and in which you can show immediate results.

Quick Hits with High Impact

– Joseph Vesey, Chief Marketing Officer at Xylem, Inc.

"Quick hits are an important way to keep leadership and sales excited and continuing to support marketing's journey. For example, we've identified some short cycle businesses and areas of opportunity, and we're building campaigns to actually close business in the first quarter. We're tying these quick hits to growth projects for visibility and results."

Getting Sales On Board

– Amy Hawthorne, B2B Revenue Marketing Leader at Rackspace

"Marketing automation technology not only promotes more accurate forecasting, it also helps salespeople better leverage CRM during the selling process," said Amy Hawthorne, B2B revenue marketing leader at Rackspace, a global provider of open cloud computing services. "Our approach has been to feed the sales team bite-sized chunks of information and activities to help them understand, embrace, and actively use the power of marketing automation and CRM."

Marketing recently enabled the sales team to use customized templates to send highly personalized and trackable messages through CRM. For example, one rep targeted a large global account, conducted research to identify key people, and used the templates provided by marketing to launch mini campaigns. As a result, the rep secured twelve meetings with this one account within thirty days!

"Now that he understands the power of technology on his own, he's eager to move to the next phase, asking marketing to help him set up templates for different audiences and develop dynamic nurture streams," Amy said.

"Our sales reps are loving this! They are seeing results and are coming to me asking, *What about this…can I do this…can I see the tracking on that?*"

At this stage, marketing is really working on alignment with sales. But true synergy only occurs once salespeople become *advocates* of revenue marketing.

Change Step #5: Advocacy

STAGES OF REVENUE MARKETING CHANGE

Disruption 〉 Resistance 〉 Acceptance 〉 Adoption 〉 **Advocacy**

At this step, sales and marketing are working together as one cohesive team. They are advocates of each other and recognize that the whole is greater than the sum of the parts. For example, once revenue targets are set, sales and marketing work together to create *one* plan for how they can reach these goals. Another characterization of advocacy is when sales approaches marketing with ideas for how they can work together to impact revenue. This is what happened for Rachel Dennis at Getty Images.

The Revenue Bridge— Country by Country

– Rachel Dennis, Director of Lead Generation and Retention at Getty Images

"At worldwide media company Getty Images, meeting sales quota is a team effort.

"To me, sales and marketing alignment is fundamental, which means that revenue marketing is aligned with the vision for sales goals," said Rachel Dennis, director of lead generation and retention at Getty

Images. "To support this, we created what we call a 'revenue bridge' for key countries that have significant growth opportunities for strategic products."

The revenue bridge is specific by country and links revenue gross targets to lead provisions based on expected volumes and conversion rates. It also ensures that the marketing resources are in place to help sales reach quota.

"It establishes how each country will meet its revenue targets by providing X number of leads with Y conversion rate and Z average order value. This way, it is firmly integrated and totally in line with the sales strategy," said Rachel.

At Getty Images, Rachel works with a team comprised of a sales leader, a product leader, a marketing leader, and business analyst to identify product opportunities by country. This team is responsible for building the revenue bridges, as well as reporting and communicating to sales.

"We provide the revenue targets, the particular lead sources and the action rates for how we will get there," said Rachel.

"And because a salesperson is leading this, there is greater buy-in from the entire sales organisation. They realize that the only way we are going to reach revenue targets is by all of us aligning to focus on these recommendations. Plus, they see exactly how marketing will help them reach their goals."

True Synergy

– Steve Valentine, VP Northern Region Acquisition Sales for PGi

"I said this in a meeting and will state it again. In my ten years of service here at PGi, I have never worked with a sharper, more focused team of marketing professionals. The alignment with sales is perfect, and the burning desire to help get revenue in the door is just so refreshing."

One final cautionary tale on getting to synergy with sales is to start where you can. This is actually a very practical approach and one provided by Fiona Nolan of CommScope.

It Doesn't Have to be Everyone Out of the Gate

– Fiona Nolan, SVP of Global Marketing for CommScope

"You are not going to get everyone on board from the beginning. Work with salespeople or sales groups who get your vision and can work to make your quick hits a success. After one presentation, our

VP of sales said to me, 'I don't think I've ever gotten so many whoops of joy over the web localization option and the revenue responsibility of 10 percent, in particular.' We are inducting some salespeople by fire and then others hear about the training and want to be involved. Some of the senior sales management team is also very enthusiastic. I wouldn't say all of them, but we align ourselves with those who are most interested first. It doesn't have to be everyone right out of the gate."

KEY PLAY

This chapter is a Playbook for creating marketing and sales synergy. Here is one Key Play to help you get started. I recommend you write this out, not just think it through.

1. Do a quick run-through of the Marketing and Sales Synergy Model:

- How well educated are you and your team on sales?

- Have you worked with sales to create one revenue language?

- How will you create vision, build a plan, and communicate?

- How will you establish shared goals?

"When I go into some of these meetings with sales or with the board to talk about marketing operations and our contribution to the business, I sound like the CFO or VP of sales. I talk about pipeline growth and closed business. This year, I have signed up to cover 55% of net new business and that cascades down through my marketing organization. They know the revenue we have to drive and where it's going to come from across our product lines, and that's what they have signed up for."

– Ken Robinson, VP of Revenue Marketing at NAVEX Global

"Once we had the data and access to the digital body language, we were able to do a regression analysis correlated to conversions. I was truly honored that we have won awards for this work. To me, our approach was very intuitive and was just the next logical step in marketing analytics. I would not have done it any other way."

– Eva Tsai, Director of Marketing Operations at Citrix

"It doesn't matter how many web leads there are, how many press releases you issue, or how many customers visit your website if none of it translates into revenue."

– Kristen Diamond, Director of Marketing Programs at ORSYP

8

METRICS THAT MATTER

It's 7:55 a.m., and you step into the elevator that will zip you up to your office. Just as the doors begin to close, in steps your CEO.

Instantly, you begin to sweat. You muster the strength to smile nonchalantly as he turns to you, smiles back, and casually asks, "So, what's going to be the highlight of the marketing report this quarter? Hopefully, some real revenue growth!"

You have to think fast. What you say next will show him what kind of fearless leader he has in front of his marketing team. Do you go with Answer #1?

"Well, hits to our website are up, we've grown our number of Twitter followers, and we have passed more leads on to sales this quarter."

Or, do you go with Answer #2?

"We grew pipeline revenue by 21 percent last quarter and increased closed business by 8 percent. We're forecasting the same for the upcoming quarter."

Which set of metrics do you think matters most to your CEO? Which answer will convince him and demonstrate that marketing is taking a true role in revenue contribution and deserves a seat at the revenue table?

If you're reading this book, I hope you chose the second answer!

EMBRACE METRICS THAT MATTER

As you begin your revenue marketing journey, you will need to embrace the idea that financial and ROI metrics are now becoming your de facto measures of success. The days of being happy with reporting a lot of activity-based metrics are over. While you will continue to track and improve activity-based measures such as open and click-through rates, your key measures of success are now in revenue and financial terms. This is what is required to move from a cost center to a revenue center.

From Cost Center to Profit Center

– Cleve Bellar, VP, Marketing – Revenue Performance Center, Sage

"I'm passionate about showing that marketing is a profit center and not a cost center. I'm passionate about when we show that we are spending money, showing how we expect to get something in return and then proving it."

In addition—and this is a key point—you will mature your measurement competency over time. Beyond time and experience, maturing your measurement competencies and skills are a function of the right mindset, goals, and technology. Patty Foley-Reid of Iron Mountain follows a revenue formula.

My Revenue Formula

– Patty Foley-Reid, Director of Inbound and Content Marketing at Iron Mountain

"My formula for impacting revenue is this: *First, you have to know the math.* Understand the lead volume, the conversion rates, and the value of those leads. *Second, you have to manage your program portfolio.* This has three parts: awareness, demand, and acceleration. *Third, you need to ignite the catalyst,* which is frankly, compelling content. Your catalyst is your unique point of view, which you integrate into your program portfolio to optimize results. This is how you gain leverage. Your personal goals for the New Year might be diet and exercise, but in the business world, it is leads and more leads. As revenue marketers, it is critical that we attach ourselves to revenue and always think about the true value we bring to the organization."

To mature your measurement competency, you need to first create an environment and a mindset for measurement by changing the focus from marketing *activities* to revenue marketing *results*. Let me give you an example. In 2004, I implemented Eloqua and Salesforce and immediately began changing the mindset of my team and how they were measured. Prior to implementing marketing automation, we were focused on creating activities: how many visitors to the website, number of people who attended an event, open and click-through rates on our e-mail programs. Our mindset was firmly and proudly based in producing a laundry list of activities. Once we began our journey to revenue marketing, this mindset shifted to results. I remember the meeting I had with my marketing team when I announced that part of their variable compensation was now based on the number of opportunities created in Salesforce as a result of our campaigns. We were in Atlanta, Georgia, and you could hear the whining all the way to Seattle, Washington! "We don't have control" was the common lament, but a funny thing happened. Once I gave them a reason to change their mindset and tied these new goals to compensation, the behavior changed fast, and we achieved our goals in the first quarter. We made the transition from being an activity-based marketing department to one producing revenue results.

Conversely, many marketing organizations today are still clinging to an activity-based mindset. Here is an example.

WHAT GETS MEASURED GETS DONE

I was recently working with a large technology company at the very beginning of its revenue marketing journey. During our session, I asked the team to give me an example of a great recent campaign.

The team proudly shared a campaign that took about three months to put into place. The campaign used e-mail with unique content and a microsite with some social aspect, all focused on one specific area of the business. It was a considerable effort from a cross-functional team.

When I asked about results from the campaign, they proudly announced they had excellent open rates and downloads of the paper. They reported on activity-based metrics: who did what to get the campaign out the door, the new content, how they used social, and finally, a few e-mail statistics.

When I further asked about results such as leads, lead to conversion, or opportunities from this campaign, they looked at me with puzzled expressions on their faces. "We don't track that," they responded.

"Can you?" I asked. They said that they could, but it would take too much work.

I then asked why they did the campaign. In other words, when they set up the campaign, what was the goal? They responded that someone asked for it, so they did it.

This marketing team was simply doing business as usual and was measured on "getting it done." They were not tasked with creating a business result, nor was this an environment for that kind of measurement. There are many reasons why.

No one in the company expected anything different from marketing—or even understood that marketing was capable of more. In addition, the marketing team did not have the right technology for closed-loop reporting. And perhaps most importantly, they had no compensation tied to doing anything differently. This team of marketers had no immediate reason to have a measurement mindset or to change their focus from activities to results.

Activity vs. Results

– Amy Hawthorne, B2B Revenue Marketing Leader at Rackspace

"Often times, marketers view production and activity as more important than the end results because they don't want to wait on the results. They don't want to invest the time to do it right. I think that's why there aren't a lot of revenue marketers out there yet. I think there are still a lot of people out there with the mindset of, *we do a lot of stuff, we get a lot of stuff out the door.* But does it matter? I don't think they know."

Mindset and goals are slightly related, but goals differ in that marketing has to have goal alignment with sales and to the revenue number in order to be successful in impacting revenue and financial metrics. Too often I find marketing is doing "their thing" and sales is doing "their thing," and they are working in opposite directions. Once you begin to help your marketing team shift their mindset to the possibilities of revenue and financial measurement, you then need to provide clear and obtainable goals for your team.

Finally, you just cannot do this without technology. Marketing automation, CRM, and other tools enable the end-to-end tracking and reporting that establishes the role of marketing in revenue…without a doubt.

WATCH YOUR LANGUAGE

Once you have the mindset, goals, and technology in motion, you'll notice your language changing also. For the revenue marketer, I find the language they use is distinctive from that of other marketers in several ways. Using this new language represents a tangible observation and data point that tells me where marketers are on the journey.

Revenue marketers universally use the language of *business*, not the language of marketing, when talking to the senior management team and the C-suite. They describe their contribution to the company (their metrics) in terms of pipeline, opportunities, and revenue. If they do talk about how many campaigns they have run or how many hits they have to the website, it is of secondary importance.

"X" In and "Y" Out

– Amy Hawthorne, B2B Revenue Marketing Leader at Rackspace

"In my very first meeting with our VP of sales, I drew a picture of a sales funnel pipeline and asked him to explain to me how things converted through the pipeline. My goal, I told him, was for marketing to work a quarter or two ahead of sales and identify a formula around *if I put in x number of leads, this is how many will ultimately convert.* He looked at me and said, *Do you really think this is possible?* I said, *I've done it before. I know it's possible.*"

The metrics they measure and talk about are *metrics that matter* to a CEO and are communicated in terms a CEO understands and can evaluate. Revenue marketers also actually talk to the CFO and work as a team on ROI.

Today's revenue marketing executives have no hesitation when asked what they measure and where they currently stand against their number. Their key metrics are always top of mind, and they can always tell you where they are in relation to their goals. They don't have to look or pull out a spreadsheet or "go into their system." These metrics are a constant driving force for their entire group every single day.

Finally, revenue marketers work hard to create a common language for all stages of a lead and the metrics across the company by working closely with sales to define all elements of lead generation—and by working with senior management to align their metrics to the company's goals and quota.

Whatever set of metrics these marketers use, they are agreed upon by sales and senior management and include a global set of definitions, deliverables, and expectations from both marketing and sales. In addition, there is clarity and understanding on when and how the metrics will be reported, and most importantly, how the person receiving the report will use the data for better decision-making.

Goal Alignment

– Kristen Wright, VP of Marketing at Pinstripe

"Rather than just set goals around how many leads go in and then leaving it up to sales to close them, we try to really reflect on the partnership between sales and marketing and commit to contributing X number of booked deals to each division annually from marketing leads. As a result, we pay closer attention to lead sources in the system and tracking opportunities throughout the entire process, because our focus is on helping the company achieve its revenue goals. Last year, we met the goals of one of our divisions and exceeded it for one. This year we have actually doubled the goals for both."

WHAT YOU MEASURE CHANGES OVER TIME

Let's talk about what you can measure and how what you measure will change over time. I'll use the Metrics That Matter on the Revenue Marketing Journey table (see fig. 8.1) as a framework for this discussion.

METRICS THAT MATTER ON THE REVENUE MARKETING JOURNEY

	Traditional	Lead Generation	Demand Generation	Revenue Marketing
Definition	Focused on numbers related to activities and is not typically involved in lead generation.	Focused on numbers related to activities. The hot new metric is how many "leads" marketing produces for sales. The definition of a lead at this point is still fuzzy and is often a creation of marketing only, with little sales involvement.	Focused on pipeline and revenue-related metrics.	RPS-Focused on pipeline and revenue-related metrics that are now *repeatable, predictable, and scalable*
Metric Categories	**Activity Reporting**	**E-mail Reporting**	**Funnel Reporting**	**Funnel Forecasting**
Sample Metrics	# of events per year	# of e-mails sent	Funnel velocity	Funnel velocity
	# of attendees at each event	Cadence of e-mail sends	# of MQLS, SALs, SQLS	# of MQLS, SALs, SQLS
	# of ad impressions	% open & % click-through	Conversion rates from Lead to MQL to SAL to SQL to close	Conversion rates from Lead to MQL to SAL to SQL to close
	# of website visitors	% bounce	% and $ amount of pipeline contributed from marketing	% and $ amount of pipeline contributed from marketing
	# of press releases	# and % of form completions	% and $ amount of revenue contributed from marketing	% and $ amount of revenue contributed from marketing
		# of "leads" sent to sales	Lead scoring	Lead scoring
		Cost per lead	Analytics and campaign/program ROI	Analytics and campaign/program ROI
Reporting	Report on activity-focusedmetrics as they occurred in the past. A manual process.	Report on activity-focused metrics as they occurred in the past with number of leads produced as the key metric. Often a manual process.	Report on funnel and revenue-focused metrics as they occurred in the past. Closed-loop reporting used to make better business decisions. An automated process.	Report on funnel and revenue-focused metrics as they occurred in the past and can now provide a marketing forecast. Closed-loop reporting used to make better business decisions. An automated process.
Technology Drivers	Marketing resource management (MRM) systems and website	E-mail systems	Marketing automation integrated with CRM. May also have other analytics tools.	Marketing automation integrated with CRM. Should have other analytics tools.

Figure 8.1

Phase 1: Traditional to Lead Generation

For a marketer moving from Traditional to Lead Generation, common metrics are what I like to call *ground zero metrics*—those metrics that help you build a foundation for the more mature metrics to come. As you review these metrics, you will notice the majority are activity-based, not results-based. These metrics might include:

- An e-mail system that is up and running

- A clean and targeted list for campaigns

- A regular cadence for campaigns

- An established baseline of conversions, including:

    o   Your open rates compared to the industry standard

    o   Your click-through rates compared to the industry standard

    o   Your form completion rates compared to the industry standard

- Documented leads

    o   Number of leads to sales

    o   Conversion of these leads to opportunities and closed business. (At this stage of the journey, this is typically a manual process, but it can be done.)

Phase 2: Lead Generation to Demand Generation

At this stage, you probably have a marketing automation system in place that is integrated with CRM. This allows for the automated, closed-loop reporting that enables marketing to effectively report on revenue metrics. As you look at these metrics, you will see that they are all revenue oriented.

All of the metrics from the Lead Generation phase, plus:

- Percent and number of leads accepted by sales

- Percent and number of opportunities created

- Percent and dollar amount of the pipeline

- Percent and dollar amount of closed business

- ROI

How Many Licks Does It Take to Get to the Center of a Tootsie Pop?

– Patty Foley-Reid, Director of Inbound and Content Marketing at Iron Mountain

"How many licks does it take to get to the center of a Tootsie Pop? In the commercial it says, 'The world may never know.' In the business world, a marketer needs to know. It is marketing's job to know precisely how many touches it takes to get to the center of a great sales opportunity. The goal is to find sales opportunities with as few touches as possible, over the shortest period of time, in the most economical way. Knowing exactly what it takes to predictably find and land big deals with a proven formula brings tremendous value to the business. Admittedly, measuring marketing influence isn't easy, but that's the revenue marketer's job—to know what it takes to predictably get to the center of great sales opportunities."

Metrics Tell the Story

– Jim Kanir, SVP of Sales and Marketing at Billtrust

At Billtrust, a billing services provider, marketing measures its contribution to revenue by the number of Sales Qualified Leads (SQLs) and Sales Accepted Leads (SALs). An SQL is defined as a lead from the marketing pipeline that is handed off to sales. Some SALs are converted to opportunities and closed business, while others are put back into the marketing pipeline for further nurturing.

Marketing tracks from the original engagement to when it converts from an MQL to an SQL and from SAL to closing. "Our metrics have shown that about 78 percent of all sales that come through have the marketing touch all over them," said Jim Kanir, SVP of sales and marketing at Billtrust. "As a result of marketing efforts, the sales team has become much more efficient and production per rep is continually increasing."

Marketing decided that the only leads that count are those that become SALs. "If the salesperson takes an SAL and says this is an opportunity I am going to pursue, then we've done our job and can now take credit for it. Marketing gets paid a bonus on SALs," Jim said.

"When I first came on board, I was assigned a dollar amount of new revenue that was 50 percent year-over-year growth from the previous year. We exceeded that goal by $500,000. The next year, they increased our goal by another 50 percent year-over-year growth rate. We exceeded that by $2.4 million. Our revenue quota has increased dramatically since the beginning."

Phase 3: Demand Generation to Revenue Marketing

When a marketer has moved from demand generation to revenue marketing, sales and marketing are closely aligned and closed-loop reporting is in place. Most importantly, marketing has clearly defined "metrics that matter" and can now accurately forecast its revenue contribution. The Revenue Marketing phase includes all the metrics from the Lead Generation and Demand Generation phases, plus:

- A well-established measurement discipline to diagnose gaps and improve performance

- Reliable measurements to repeat and forecast marketing performance with confidence

- The ability for operations to scale high-performance marketing

- Optimized processes and systems to allow for forecasting

- Predictive analytics

- ROI

Boardroom Credibility with Predictive Analytics

– Eva Tsai, Senior Director of Marketing Operations at Citrix

Eva Tsai does not have the typical marketer's background.

She began her career as an engineer and a consultant and, as a result, has always been focused on process and analytics. So when she decided to

177

try her hand at marketing, she wanted to know how leads move through the pipeline, and *why*, so that she could accurately forecast revenue.

As the new director of marketing operations at Citrix, she realized that analytics was key in establishing credibility to facilitate alignment between sales and marketing.

Eva began by taking a hard look at the data. Though Citrix had a marketing automation platform in place, they did not have a global lead scoring model. She studied the process and saw that how leads were being developed was not very scientific.

Eva brought in an analytics resource, and together they began work on predictive modeling. They looked back at the past four years of data—including millions of records—and analyzed it to figure out every single touch point, profile, and behavior attribute, and how that would eventually correlate to a prospect's propensity to buy.

Then, based on this analysis, they created a "myth busters" slide deck that dispelled many of the theories in place around what lead scoring really meant.

"Many of the things we thought made sense from a lead scoring perspective—like authoritative job titles, for example—no longer applied to all segments of the business, so it was very illuminating to the sales team," said Eva.

Eva's team developed a scoring algorithm based on their findings and shared it with Citrix's global sales team. They also ran simulations to confirm that it worked. Using their algorithm, they predicted that they would improve the marketing lead-to-opportunity conversion rate by 16 to 24 percent, with 20 percent as the most likely scenario. They released the algorithm into production in summer 2012.

"We recently analyzed the data for the quarter. Not only did the conversion rate improve as we expected, but it came in right on target. Our current improvement is 20.6 percent."

MARKETING AUTOMATION CREATES METRICS THAT MATTER

Revenue marketers not only report and forecast on metrics that matter, they also can measure competitive advantage as a result of their revenue marketing initiative. All of this is enabled by marketing automation integrated with CRM.

To gain additional understanding around what today's B2B revenue marketer is measuring, the impact they're making on competitive advantage, and the role of marketing automation in these results, let's look at the "2012 B2B Lead Generation Measurement & ROI Study" by Lenskold Group and The Pedowitz Group.

Lenskold Group conducted the online survey research with 374 marketing professionals from a cross-section of companies that covered diverse industries and ranged in size from SMB to enterprise corporations. The study analyzed three categories of marketers:

1. Marketers not using any marketing automation (no automation).

2. Marketers using marketing automation but not integrated with a CRM system (non-integrated marketing automation).

3. Marketers using marketing automation integrated with a CRM system (integrated marketing automation).

Point One: Companies Using Integrated Marketing Automation are More Likely to Report ROI and Revenue-Based Metrics.

Figure 8.2 depicts eight metric types and shows the differences in use across the three types of marketers. With only one exception (perception metrics), companies using integrated marketing automation are more likely to use metrics that matter.

METRICS USED

Which of the following metrics do you use to manage marketing performance?
(check all that apply)   (n=112,71,190)

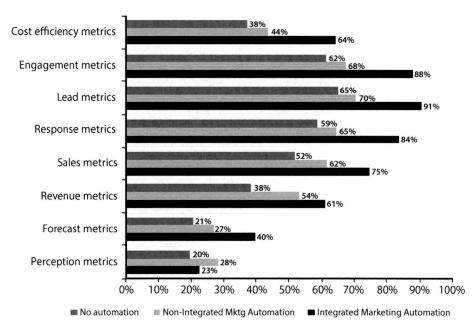

Source: "2012 B2B Lead Generation Measurement & ROI Study" by the Lenskold Group

Figure 8.2

Point Two: Marketing Automation Makes it Increasingly Easier to Track and Evaluate a Company's Marketing Efforts.

Figure 8.3 shows the increasing progression of ROI metric use when moving from no automation to fully integrated marketing automation. Marketers with integrated marketing automation (45%) are far more likely to be tracking ROI metrics than those who do not have automation (24%) or those who have automation but not integration (31%).

USERS OF INTEGRATED MARKETING AUTOMATION ARE MORE LIKELY TO CALCULATE ROI

Does your firm calculate marketing profitability, ROI (return on investment), or a similar financial measure to assess marketing effectiveness?
(Choose one)   (n=106, 70 186)

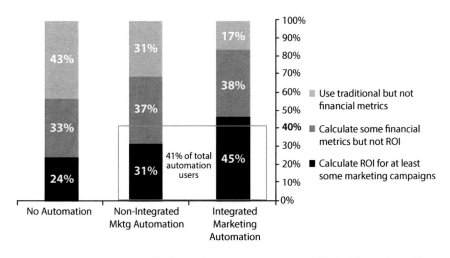

Source: "2012 B2B Lead Generation Measurement & ROI Study" by the Lenskold Group

Figure 8.3

181

Point Three: Companies with Integrated Marketing Automation are Outgrowing the Competition.

Wouldn't you like to show how, based partly on your revenue marketing efforts, your company is outgrowing the competition? This business impact number was a key finding from the study and one we will continue to measure. The revenue and financial benefits of marketing automation follow an incremental progression as marketers move from no automation to non-integrated automation (have marketing automation, but it is not integrated with CRM) and then to integrated marketing automation (see fig. 8.4). Integrated marketing automation users are experiencing greater growth (66%) compared to those with just marketing automation (58%) or no automation (50%).

USERS OF INTEGRATED MARKETING AUTOMATION REPORT GREATER GROWTH THAN COMPETITORS

How would you describe your firm's expected growth in the upcoming year relative to your primary competitors?
(n=112, 71 190)

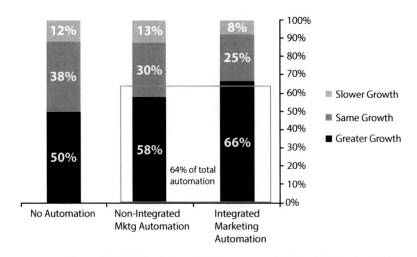

Source: "2012 B2B Lead Generation Measurement & ROI Study" by the Lenskold Group

Figure 8.4

Point Four: Higher Growth Companies Have Automation and an ROI Measurement Discipline.

The study reported that companies *outgrowing their competitors* are:

- more likely to use integrated marketing automation (57% vs. 43% of slower/same growth companies);

- more likely to have experienced an increase in total marketing revenue contribution from marketing automation (55% vs. 31% of slower/same growth companies); and

- more likely to calculate ROI to assess marketing effectiveness (41% vs. 28% of slower/same growth companies).

You can see from the 2012 Lenskold Survey that measurement is a fast-growing competency in marketing and what gets measured, gets done. You can also see that revenue marketing makes a business impact beyond a closed sale—it also demonstrably creates competitive advantage in the market.

HALLMARK OF A REVENUE MARKETER

The hallmark of a **revenue marketer** is establishing a culture of financial measurement that produces RPS—repeatable, predictable, and scalable revenue growth. Revenue marketers establish a mindset and an environment of measurement. They align marketing goals to this new reality, focus on metrics that matter, speak in terms of the business, and have earned a seat at the revenue table. Finally, revenue marketers realize that measurement is a competency that will grow and improve over time and that being held accountable for revenue is here to stay.

KEY PLAYS

This chapter identified key metrics tracked and reported on by revenue marketers. Here are four Key Plays to get you on track.

1. Identify where you are on the revenue marketing journey in regards to metrics. Use the Metrics That Matter chart (see fig. 8.1) provided in this chapter.

2. Establish and document your current measurement baseline:

- What do you measure today? Be very specific.

    o   What activities do you measure?

    o   What results do you measure?

    o   How much effort is required?

- What can you measure today? Be very specific.

    o   What activities can you measure?

    o   What results can you measure?

    o   How much effort is required?

3. Establish what metrics matter to the executive team:

- What metrics do you show to the executive team?

- What metrics do they ask for?

- What does the executive team do with these metrics?

4. Identify your measurement gaps and plan how to address these gaps:

- What are you going to do differently to move to the next level of metrics? (PS, it will be something different!)

- What difference will this make to your company?

- What happens if you can't report metrics that matter?

" We sold the concept of marketing automation and revenue marketing to the leadership team in bite-sized chunks. We then brought together forty to fifty people from around the globe who were directly related to either a marketing leader or a high influencer. For two days, we held a global summit on the fundamentals of revenue marketing. They bought in right away. They then went back to their own teams—whether in a product division or selling region—and convinced their leadership that we needed to do this. "

– Shawnn Smark, Head of Group Marketing at Bio-Rad

" This will be a long journey—it's not going to happen overnight, and some businesses may never get there. But I do believe that the majority of businesses will see the light. There will be changes and refinements along the way, and it will require champions and facilitators across each of the businesses to really get people on board and make it work. "

– Lawrence DiCapua, Leader of GE's Revenue Marketing Center of Excellence

" The next frontier is trying to figure out how to interweave all the elements of marketing together into the overall revenue performance management model and being able to tell that story. There is no silver bullet; it's about what is right for your organization and getting executives to buy in so they are in the ark with you as you're crossing the water. "

– Cleve Bellar, VP, Marketing – Revenue Performance Center, Sage

9

SELLING THE VISION

Okay, you get it, but does anyone else? Do you have the political clout to get the senior management team to listen? And if you can get them to listen, can you present a business case and financial model showing a different way to grow top-line revenue, have marketing demonstrate ROI, and do both while creating competitive advantage in the market?

How you sell the vision for revenue marketing in your company will vary based on the culture of your organization and the amount of influence and power within marketing. From meetings, to experiences, to formal three-to-five-year business models, I'll share how three different companies sold their vision for revenue marketing.

Selling the vision starts with speaking the language of executives—saving money, growing top-line revenue, and building shareholder value. In addition, executives need to see the vision, and they need to see a plan. Sally Lowery, serial Revenue Marketer, understands this well.

I'd Like to Own Some Revenue, Please

– Sally Lowery, Senior Director of Marketing for Appia

Sally Lowery is a serial revenue marketing leader who has made the transformational journey with three different companies.

When Sally works with a new company looking to transform its traditional marketing organization from a cost center into a revenue marketing machine, she goes straight to the C-level executives, looks them in the eyes, and starts the conversation with, "I'd like to own some revenue, please."

"For me, it's taking that ownership, which is scary. I know that I'm either going to do really well, or I'm going to do really poorly. But bottom line, I know I will have had some impact on whether we do, or don't, hit our goals," says Sally, senior director of marketing for Appia.

What's important to the C-level? Revenue. What's important for them to hear? That all of their leadership team is on board with driving that forward. Why? Because if you are serious about revenue marketing transformation, getting alignment with sales, marketing and the executive team is the first step to selling the vision and getting executive buy-in.

"When you take responsibility for revenue, it's a very different conversation than *we want to buy this marketing automation system and put out these campaigns*," said Sally. "I don't talk about leads anymore with sales—I talk about *revenue* and how to meet our joint acquisition and revenue goals. As you get that alignment with sales, everyone is speaking the same language and sharing the same goal. Then the vision is more easily accepted at the C-level, and everyone gets really excited about it."

You must be able to look at the sales cycle and see where marketing can most effectively create pipeline for the sales organization. This means building a team that can generate leads and actually drive opportunity value through compelling nurture and acceleration programs.

"Instead of marketing saying, *we drove a lot of leads this month*, we're saying, *we see gaps in the pipeline and here are the specific programs we'll be launching to address these gaps and help drive sales performance (quota)*," said Sally.

Alignment and buy-in are the critical first steps, but you also have to have a game plan.

"I think a game plan is sometimes what we marketers are fundamentally lacking," Sally said. "We get excited about revenue marketing—we catch the fever—but then we don't actually think about everything we need and what is required to put it all in place. We don't take the time, or we just don't know how to operationalize revenue marketing. Marketing automation technology is just one piece—it's not a silver bullet. You have to look at the broader landscape and figure out all of the components to make it work."

You can bet that got their attention. What about you? Do you feel comfortable asking your senior executive team, "May I own some revenue?" Whichever way you choose to begin that first meeting, we've worked with enough companies to know that there is more than one way to sell the vision of revenue marketing.

Here is a story of how one company sold the vision to its global sales and executive team by having them *experience* revenue marketing first hand.

UNDERCOVER MARKETERS

I was recently asked to speak at a national sales meeting. Attendees included the senior leadership team, marketing leadership, sales leadership, and the entire sales force.

The VP of marketing knew that the company needed a revenue marketing initiative aimed at revenue growth. He also knew that he had to sell the vision to senior management and the sales team. In the weeks leading up to the meeting, I helped marketing go undercover to run a "secret" digital campaign specially designed for the meeting attendees.

Using marketing automation, we created a microsite that offered various assets for the upcoming meeting, including event activities and an agenda. We also set up and ran a communication campaign around the event that included lead scoring and tracking of each registered attendee's online activity for two weeks prior to the meeting. The purpose of the campaign was to have this group of executives and salespeople experience the power of marketing automation and revenue marketing through the automation flows and the digital insight provided.

During the conference, the VP of marketing made a presentation about the importance of revenue marketing to the future of the company. To prove his point, he then revealed that marketing had been running an undercover experiment on the participants and described how they had been tracking each person's online activities for the past two weeks.

By sharing the campaign results and highlighting various online activities of key executives (including the CEO), the VP was able to help this audience understand the value of revenue marketing for their organization. He even gave out awards to the hottest leads (highest lead scores).

The experiment was designed to help the attendees understand the power of revenue marketing and its importance to the company as a revenue strategy. It was a huge success and revenue marketing was adopted by the company.

BUILDING A FORMAL BUSINESS CASE FOR REVENUE MARKETING

Revenue marketing is *transformational*. This means it requires change, and change requires budget, so you have to be able to sell it. In many cases, taking the time to build and present a revenue marketing business case with a three-to-five-year financial model will get the attention and buy-in required from senior executives. This is hard work and may be out of your comfort zone, but the results are well worth the investment.

By building a formal business case for revenue marketing, you will gain additional, very important benefits.

- First, a revenue marketing business case will get the serious attention of your executive team in a way that no other format can. A business case speaks their language and provides a format that allows them to more easily make decisions for the business.

- Second, the creation of any substantial revenue marketing business case requires the interactions of functions across the company—marketing, sales, and finance (and maybe a few others). This creates understanding and buy-in, while beginning to build alignment for revenue marketing across key constituents. Executives want to see this alignment as they evaluate any new business plan.

- Third, presenting a business case allows you to define and visually depict the revenue marketing game plan, benefits, and revenue impact *over an extended period of time*. Revenue marketing is a multi-year journey for many organizations. Setting the expectation that this is not a "one and done" project, but rather, is a revenue-focused change management process occurring over time, is critical.

- Fourth, by taking the time to create a formal three-to-five-year revenue marketing business case, you are demonstrating business acumen and an understanding of the overall business dynamics of the company. In some organizations, this would be a breath of fresh air coming from marketing and would be very welcome.

SIX COMPONENTS FOR A REVENUE MARKETING BUSINESS CASE

In our experience, there are **six key components** required for building a successful revenue marketing business case. This is our framework for how to get it done and who needs to be involved.

The six components are:

1. Build alignment

2. Conduct a marketing audit

3. Visualize the opportunity

4. Plan the road map

5. Build the model

6. Measure success

SIX COMPONENTS OF A BUSINESS CASE

 **1. Build Alignment**

 **2. Conduct a Marketing Audit**

 **3. Visualize the Opportunity**

 **4. Plan the Roadmap**

 **5. Build the Model**

 **6. Measure Success**

Component #1:
Build Alignment

Without alignment, you are dead in the water. Revenue marketing requires you to create alignment, relationships, and advocacy across all key constituents affected by revenue marketing. It's never too early to begin this alignment process. Start by considering the benefits of revenue marketing for each key constituent. Write them down. This makes the process more real and helps you better organize your thoughts. Then, as you go through the formal business planning process, you will want to tweak and validate these benefits.

Your list might include:

- Executive Leadership Team: What is the value proposition to the company? What is going to change and why now?

- CMO/VP of Marketing: Are we ready? Do we have alignment? Will we have a closed loop?

- EVP of Sales: What is the revenue impact? How soon? How much effort?

- Campaign Staff: What is my role? Will it do what I want? Will it be ready in time?

- CIO/IT Director: Can you use what we have? What do you need from IT? What about integration?

- Sales Team: Is this a corporate project? How will this help *me*? What is revenue marketing?

- MarCom Staff: Do I have to change? What about the newsletter? What about my funding?

- Partners: Will I see more leads? Will I have visibility? Is there closed-loop reporting?

- Sales Operations: What changes in CRM? What is a joint pipeline? Will sales use this?

One way to build early alignment for revenue marketing is to use a cross-functional team to create the business case. This was the approach used by Sage.

Cross-Functional Team

– Nancy Harris, VP and General Manager, Sage, Revenue Marketing University Webinar

"At Sage, we had a project charter and kicked off with a fairly high-level program objective associated with it, which was to better optimize for building a dominant master brand and better optimize our North America marketing efforts.

We created a cross-functional team representing different business units ranging from sales, marketing, IT, legal, and finance, and a chair was picked for the group.

We started with ongoing meetings and discussions around the 'big idea' and what would meet that objective. Through group meetings, e-mails, and one-on-one meetings, we began to take that core group and build outward to sales and marketing constituents. Eventually, we were able to gain buy-in across all business units and functional areas."

Designing the makeup of the cross-functional team responsible for creating the revenue marketing business plan is a key milestone. This group will need to meet regularly and will be charged with key deliverables while they are still doing their day jobs. In addition, communicating this team's activities throughout the process will further enable alignment across a broader portion of the company.

Don't try to hide the activities of this group. A certain level of transparency reduces system-wide anxiety around the possible changes to marketing.

Component #2:
Conduct a Marketing Audit

Knowing the facts and establishing the baseline for change builds credibility in your revenue marketing business case. The baseline is developed as a result of a full marketing audit.

To build a financial case for revenue marketing, the marketing audit needs to encompass different business divisions, different customer acquisition models and sales cycles, different solutions, different internal systems, and different marketing organizations (field, corporate, business unit, etc.). The marketing audit needs to detail current marketing spend and current marketing return, as well as key funnel metrics and processes. Understanding your marketing spend is important because this initiative should drive improvements in spend, which ultimately drives revenue effectiveness and will become a foundational element for the business case throughout. Understanding spend will also help you determine how to reallocate funds if you are building this business case in the middle of the year.

Understanding current funnel metrics will help establish the baseline for your financial scenarios. For example, if you know that your MQL to SAL conversion rate is 32 percent, you can calculate the revenue improvement based on the conversion rate moving to 35 percent or 40 percent. One customer example was the customer win-back rate—a well-established number in the company. Increasing this number by a few percentage points would have a major impact on revenue and at the same time address a major pain in the company. This number, the estimated improvement, and resulting revenue were actually incorporated into the business plan and approved.

Another client sent out a survey to each business unit and asked them to describe their funnel stages and conversions along the funnel. They also looked for any metrics already in the system they could use to create a baseline in the selling the vision pitch to the North America executive team. Such metrics included e-mail open and click-through rates, form conversion rates, and how these metrics changed when using a nurture campaign approach versus a batch-and-blast approach. All of these numbers were incorporated into the plan and approved by executives as a relevant baseline.

The marketing audit should also include a skills inventory for revenue marketing, which is a unique set of skills. Understanding the skills you already have—versus skills you do not have—will help you shape the business case in terms of headcount, budget, and timing. Revenue marketing skills are a critical element to baseline.

Many times, clients will neglect this stage of building a baseline around their skills and metrics because of time, money, or motivation. We strongly suggest every company take this approach. A good marketing audit will not just find numbers but will identify opportunities to make the business case viable while identifying quick wins once the plan is accepted.

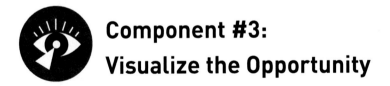

Component #3: Visualize the Opportunity

Those projects that gain alignment and build momentum are led by marketers who can crystallize a tangible revenue marketing vision. The most effective way to visualize the opportunity is by creating financial scenarios based on funnel metrics. Determining weak spots in the funnel and in marketing processes that can be addressed by revenue marketing is a good place to start. The data used to visualize the opportunity is typically derived from the marketing audit.

THE FUNNEL IS ALL ABOUT CONVERSIONS

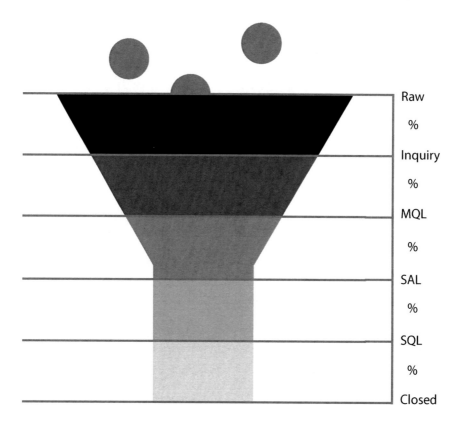

Using the funnel as your guide, build several financial return scenarios and show the impact of even small changes in various conversion metrics. Build assumptions based on particulars from your business environment. You will find that opportunities for improvement as a result of revenue marketing will be in many places.

For example, one company I worked with offered trials of their software. They had a large number of participants, yet they only saw a 1 percent conversion rate from trial to close—well below industry average. Once someone signed up for a trial, they entered the system as a lead (the stage before an MQL). This company did not have the systems to track lead activity in the trial, nor did they have a way to automatically route qualified leads to sales. As part of the business case exercise, we showed an increase in trial closes from 1 percent to 3 percent by using marketing automation to track and respond to lead behavior during the trial and to notify sales in real time once the lead became sales ready. This one line item in the business case addressed a major pain in the company and provided a 10x ROI for investing in revenue marketing.

Think in terms of specific areas of weakness in your funnel and how even minor improvements can have an impact on revenue. Find those areas in the funnel where leads and customers are leaking out of the system and focus on those first. This will help you gain business credibility, provide you with some strong financial scenarios, and provide quick wins once your plan is accepted.

Build a few revenue/efficiency scenarios based on identified business problems in the company and then show the impact of revenue marketing. Typical scenarios include:

- Deep in funnel leakage (like the trial software example above)

  o Leads lost in trials

  o Leads lost at the SAL stage

  o Leads at the SQL stage

  o Leads lost to competitor

  o Leads stuck (not moving, needs an automatic nudge)

- Retention programs

  o Runs automatically, with minimal time and effort from sales or marketing

- Upsell/cross-sell current clients

  o If a client buys X, place in automatic nurture campaign to get them to buy Y in three months

- Do more with same

  o Same size marketing team, making a revenue impact

  o Same size marketing team, executing more events, with better results

- o Same size marketing team, executing more campaigns, with better results

- o Same size sales team, driving more revenue

- o Same sales team, with higher quota per rep

- o Get new reps up to quota, quicker

- o Website conversions

These scenarios should illustrate a predictable way to impact revenue and/or improve efficiencies. Remember to whom you are selling and what interests them the most. What interests the CFO may differ from what interests the CEO.

What a CFO Likes

– Nancy Harris, VP and General Manager, Sage, Revenue Marketing University Webinar

"This is where our CFO really lit up because he could see, 'Wow—I can have a predictable, reliable way to forecast, and if I invest, incremental revenue will flow.' This was a very compelling visual with the associated numbers."

Component #4:
Plan the Road Map

Once you have the opportunities identified, how are you going to get there? The road map begins the discussion and visualization around the movement to revenue marketing.

You may be in the traditional marketing, lead generation, or early on in the demand generation stage of the journey, but you still need to outline what needs to happen to drive change and move to the next stage.

This planning includes the strategy, people, process, results, content, and technology elements you will need on your revenue marketing journey. For each, think through what needs to happen. Identify priorities and outline how to sequence next steps. How long will it take to enable? What skills are needed? How soon will you realize results? Planning and timing are critically important to the development of your model.

RM6 Self-Analysis

– Nancy Harris, VP and General Manager, Sage, Revenue Marketing University Webinar

"We held a workshop that helped us take the RM6 self-analysis and really drive down into each of the areas. For example, we had different CRM systems in place across different business units. For each element, we walked through where we were today and what we needed to do to enable a Revenue Marketing Center of Excellence.

> We started with technology and decided that we couldn't go to market with a single voice until we were all on the same page there. We created a clear map of where we needed to go."

Show what you will do in the first thirty/sixty/ninety days, including the campaigns that will be in place, as well as the results from the website, lead scoring tools, and the timing of revenue.

Component #5: Build the Model

It is now time to model expected sales pipeline improvements based on your scenarios. Show revenue improvement streams around specific geography, product, service, campaigns, and improvements in conversion rates through the funnel. How much revenue will be attributed to this initiative?

Build a few simple summaries to bring it all together to tell the story. It is one thing to show a change in the funnel that will bring X in additional revenue, but a CFO or the executives who are looking to fund this project are going to want a complete, holistic picture that brings together the revenue, cost, investment, timing, and how it is going to happen.

Look at total revenue that will be improved. This is the target you are going after, but how quickly will this be realized? There is a learning curve and a ramp-up stage in getting your team up to speed. Build that into your model so that you are not overstating the benefits.

Remember to offset those improvements in revenue. What is the required investment? Think in terms of data, marketing automation, skills training, or investing in more content. Where are the spend categories? How much of this will be a one-time, upfront investment, and what are the ongoing sustaining costs? Make sure you highlight all of this, as it is an important part of building the business case.

Also, are there any offsets? Are there any costs that will go away? Can you retire any applications? Are there internal charges from IT that may go away once you have your own self-contained marketing automation tools? Capture those. Are there any joint marketing funds you received that can now be used to offset some of these investments to deploy revenue marketing? What are the net costs? Net cash flows? Is it a compelling story to present to your executives?

Component #6: Measure Success

Executives want to see revenue accountability, so you need to plan for it, enable it, and build the business case around it. Executive teams, as well as partners that are providing funding, want to measure and see the success. The goal is closed-loop reporting enabled by marketing automation and CRM.

When you present your business case, think through how you are going to measure success. Are you going to measure success by the number of leads being generated? By the quality of those leads? Spend time thinking through the metrics—the financial, operational impacts that you are making—but also measure progress. Measure success by building the competencies around strategy, people, process, technology, data, programs, content, and results.

What are the key competencies needed to drive results and success? Which are in place today, and which are you working on? Which are focused on proposed projects you are laying out in the business case? Which competencies are important but still further out? Which competencies are you trying to address immediately?

A successful business case begins with building alignment, and you gain that alignment by presenting a very visual picture of the opportunities. Know the facts and—like any business case—don't try to build it out until you have a plan (the road map).

Know *exactly* what you are proposing so that you can honestly relay the cost, timing, and revenue that will be impacted and be able to build a model that reflects that.

And finally, have a plan not only to get funding, but also to measure success. When you measure success, you are then able to look at it, review it, evaluate it, and optimize it.

From simple to complex, the type of business case you'll need to build will be based on the business case process your company uses. Some are very formal and require a three-to-five-year set of projections for costs and revenues. Others are as simple as a face-to-face meeting to discuss the initiative. The point is this: find out how your company makes financial decisions and how they approach unique projects, and then build your case to fit within those parameters.

KEY PLAY

This chapter presented numerous ways to sell the vision for revenue marketing and gain executive buy-in. In one example, I detailed the six components that can be used as your Playbook for building a formal business case and financial model. Regardless of the method you choose, here is one Key Play to help you get started. I recommend you write this out, not just think it through.

1. Do a quick run-through of the formal business case:

   - Write out how you would respond to each of the six components presented in the chapter.

"Innovation distinguishes between a leader and a follower."

– Steve Jobs

10

WHAT'S NEXT IN THE REVENUE MARKETING PLAYBOOK?

Imagine an organization in which every marketer in your organization:

- understands the concept and value of revenue marketing;

- shares a common revenue marketing language; and

- is measured on business results, not just activities.

Imagine an organization in which:

- marketers are accountable for revenue-related metrics;

- marketing and sales enjoy a synergistic relationship characterized by common goals and incentive plans;

- revenue marketing technologies are optimized and serve as the backbone for transformation; and

- the global Revenue Marketing Center of Excellence is optimized at the corporate level and across geographies and business units.

Imagine an organization in which marketing has transformed from a cost center to a revenue center.

This vision for revenue marketing is a game changer, and while few companies have achieved this full vision (especially at the enterprise and global level), many have started the journey and *many* more are beginning the journey every day. The amount of change in this space is rapid and continues to accelerate as marketers become more experienced in all the aspects of revenue marketing and as the technology continues to evolve.

Within this dynamic environment, I want to dedicate this last chapter to my observations of what is next for revenue marketing with the full expectation that these observations may seem out of date pretty quickly. I hope so and look forward to updating and sharing new information, case studies, and ideas for the marketing executive's revenue marketing Playbook.

I believe there are five key drivers for revenue marketing that will continue to be game changers for organizations now and moving forward.

1. Evolving role of the CMO

2. Education

3. Technology

4. Innovation

5. Globalization

EVOLVING ROLE OF THE CMO

The role and expectations of today's B2B CMO are changing dramatically. In Chapter 1, I mentioned the Global CMO study conducted by IBM that showed key CMO measurements for the future included marketing ROI, customer experience, conversion rate/new customers, overall sales, marketing-influenced sales, revenue per customer, and finally social media metrics. Five of the seven metrics have to do with revenue. The days of the CMO running a pure cost center are over.

Given this shift in CMO responsibility, it would seem that revenue marketing would be an important part of the CMO mission and vision. Yet, I rarely see the office of the CMO in enterprise companies directly involved in revenue marketing. More often, I see a business unit alone or a vice president who is one to three levels below the CMO actually taking the initiative to spearhead revenue marketing in an organization. I believe this is a strategic mistake, given the market changes I have discussed in this book. Change is slow at any executive level, and it typically takes some powerful forces for it to occur. In this situation, I see that a combination of business disruption, technology disruption, changing client behavior, and new, more tech-savvy marketers will continue to force change at the CMO level. Technology especially is and will continue to be a key driver of change in this role. Any successful CMO in the B2B space will need to be well-versed in using technology to help create and execute strategy. I also believe that CMOs who do this *now* will gain an early competitive advantage, will enjoy longer tenure, and will have more power on the executive team.

You'll be hearing a lot more from me about how the CMO role is influenced by revenue marketing.

EDUCATION

Education is largely an unrecognized issue in revenue marketing that is costly in terms of time, efficiency, and impact on revenue. I'm often surprised at how many marketing executives buy into the revenue marketing strategy yet do not understand what it takes to enable their team to be successful. They don't fully understand the need to commit time, money, and resources for education, training, and best practices. Yes, you can get training on how to run a marketing automation system, and many vendors do this for free. Yes, you can get e-mail/lead generation/demand generation best practices, and many vendors also do this for free. This is all excellent information, but it is being consumed and used in an ad hoc manner across organizations. It does not take into account each unique and dynamic business environment or provide one holistic set of standards for a company.

As companies begin the revenue marketing journey, taking an ad hoc approach to education and training will be insufficient. It would be like asking the sales team to switch from product sales to solution sales with no training and no organizational adjustment. In changing a sales team from tactical to strategic, there are several key factors that would also apply in changing marketing to revenue marketing.

First, there is recognition that the sales team may need to be reorganized, as some team members are not cut out for this new role and must be replaced. In conjunction with team reorganization, there will need to be new goals and a new compensation structure. Next, there will be training in new processes, new techniques, new best practices, and new technology. As sales takes on a new role, there will be other organizational adjustments required in services and marketing. Finally, no one expects this to happen overnight. Rather, this strategic transformation is forecasted over an extended period of time.

You are asking marketing to make the same magnitude of change without providing the tools, the training/education, and the environment required for success.

I am just beginning to see a change to this ad hoc educational approach. As this market rapidly matures, more companies are realizing the magnitude of change and what is required to fully enable it. They are beginning to look at more comprehensive education, training, and best practices plans. We have worked with a number of companies to develop and deliver broad and comprehensive revenue marketing curricula. For one company, we are providing revenue marketing education to their partner ecosystem to improve channel loyalty and productivity. In addition, we find a few leading companies are finding value in a revenue marketing certification process. I see a lot more of this in the future.

Education, training, and best practices are essential to enabling the switch to revenue marketing. Companies that take this enablement approach and dedicate the necessary resources will be ahead of the competition.

Look for my updates on how enterprise organizations are adopting more formal training and education practices for optimized revenue marketing.

TECHNOLOGY

I have three points to make about technology.

First, let's face it. Technology is the game changer for marketing, and this will continue. The savvy CMO and team will stay abreast of the latest technologies to further improve their revenue marketing practice. Not doing so will put the CMO's job in jeopardy as well as the competitive position of the company.

Second, the pervasive use of technology by marketing has led to the formation of operations groups that are owned and run by marketing. I vividly remember our first client that had a marketing operations group (2007) and thought how innovative it was that marketing owned their technology framework. It made sense in that customer environment but still represented a big departure from the typical structure in which IT owns everything related to technology. Since then, I've seen more and more successful revenue marketers implement and own marketing's technology framework. They are now in the best position to blend their knowledge of the technology, strategy, and process to drive revenue results. This is a trend that will continue.

Third, as marketing uses more technology, in more strategic ways, the rise of a Marketing Technology Officer (MTO) will be an interesting role to watch. This is currently a topic of much conversation among analysts and marketing leaders. The primary idea behind this role is that all customer-facing technologies should report to marketing as they have a better understanding of customers than IT. The role is also supported by the fact that newer technologies (software-as-a-service) do not require legions of IT staff to keep systems running or to make changes.

Whether it's a formal MTO role or a less formal structure, the idea of IT reporting to marketing is growing. I recently attended a national conference and heard Motorola's case study on their revenue marketing journey. In their organization, IT reports to the office of the CMO. You could have heard a pin drop when they shared this information!

Technology is rapidly evolving and changing the role of the CMO and the role of marketing. Successful CMOs will start now to transform their traditional environments to ones that embrace and optimize technology as a business driver.

As revenue marketing technology continues to evolve and affect marketing's role in the business, I'll continue to comment and share new trends.

INNOVATION

I want to say a word or two about innovation, as I believe that revenue marketing is innovation. Broadly defined, innovation means new ideas or new ways to compete and prosper. Innovation might occur through a product, technology, service, process, or a combination of factors.

I see revenue marketing as an innovation driven by technology, changes in the market, and changes in customer behavior. While I have not seen a company embrace revenue marketing formally from the office of innovation (if they have one), I have heard many VPs of marketing use language describing their revenue marketing efforts as a new way to compete and prosper. Perhaps because revenue marketing is a strategy coming from the marketing group, who are not traditionally known for business innovation, it receives less attention than it deserves. As marketing learns to speak the language of business, revenue marketing will gain adoption as an innovative way to compete in the market.

It will be interesting to see how the strategy and innovation of revenue marketing plays out. You will be hearing a lot more from me on this topic.

GLOBALIZATION

Revenue marketing was first adopted by smaller, more agile companies as they were deploying marketing automation systems. The technology was easy to implement, the marketing department was small, and it was easy (comparatively speaking) to make a revenue impact. The market learned a lot from these early pioneers.

Now, as more and more enterprise companies with global operations are working to implement and optimize revenue marketing, they are finding it is not as straightforward as launching multiple campaigns in multiple languages. They are learning it requires a new level of effort and coordination to create best practices, programs, templates, processes, content, and standards on a global level, while keeping the in-country or in-region differences intact. In addition, doing all of this to create a repeatable, predictable, and scalable impact on global revenue brings an entire new level of complexity to revenue marketing.

I do see a handful of highly innovative and competitive companies in the early to middle stages of revenue marketing globalization, companies going beyond campaigns in multiple languages. These companies are spending a lot of time listening, educating, and communicating while involving multiple roles and regions. They are making long-term plans (multi-year) while focusing on short-term quick wins to help the organization learn and grow. In addition, they are setting up an environment in which best practices created at regional levels are vetted, approved, and then shared globally.

I believe these leading companies who are actively engaged in globalizing revenue marketing will be the best practice leaders for the market and, in the process, create a position of competitive differentiation for themselves.

We are currently immersed in working with several major companies who are in the process of globalizing revenue marketing. As we guide these companies on their revenue marketing journey, I look forward to sharing key learnings and best practices.

BON VOYAGE!

I hope this book has provided you a context for, and a vision of, revenue marketing in your organization. I believe this new role for marketing is one of the most exciting and game changing innovations we've ever seen in our industry. Is it hard? Yes. Does it happen overnight? No. Is it worth it? Yes.

As a forward-thinking B2B marketing leader, take the ideas, models, stories, and best practices presented in this book and use them as your personal Playbook. You can use this to help accelerate where you are or to begin your own revenue marketing journey. Now you have the framework. The vision and passion required to take the next step of the journey are up to you.

And finally, as you embark on your journey, I would love to hear your comments and your stories! Visit my blog, *Rise of the Revenue Marketer*, at www.pedowitzgroup.com/riseoftherevenuemarketer or connect with me on LinkedIn and visit my LinkedIn Group, *Rise of the Revenue Marketer*.

ABOUT THE AUTHOR

DEBBIE QAQISH, PRINCIPAL AND CHIEF STRATEGY OFFICER, THE PEDOWITZ GROUP

A nationally recognized thought leader and innovator in Revenue Marketing, Debbie Qaqish has dedicated her career to helping marketers answer the burning question of *what to do about revenue*. A true marketing revolutionary, she literally coined the term defining today's new revenue-focused marketer—the Revenue Marketer.

Her firm, The Pedowitz Group—of which she is Chief Strategy Officer and a principal—is the world's largest full-service Revenue Marketing Agency with more than 1,100 customers. As Chief Strategy Officer, Debbie maintains a thought leadership role in revenue marketing that helps to better define and shape this fast-growing and ever-changing space. In addition, Debbie actively works with many executives as they are leading the transformation of marketing from cost center to revenue center status.

Backed by twenty-five years of sales and marketing expertise, Debbie is a pioneer in marketing automation and revenue marketing—first as an early adopter of the technology in 2005, and now as an advocate and expert. She is a frequent speaker, educator, blogger, and widely published writer on the issues facing executives as they lead revenue marketing change.

Before joining The Pedowitz Group, an Inc. 500 company, Debbie served as the VP of marketing, VP of sales, and VP of strategy for several award-winning education and technology companies.

Under her leadership, The Pedowitz Group has brought to market revenue marketing models, frameworks, and tools that are helping many global clients along their journey to revenue marketing. Intellectual property examples include Revenue Marketing, the Revenue Marketing Journey, Revenue Marketing University, and the RM6.

Her other professional achievements include being a:

- widely published author in industry outlets including FierceCMO, AMA, DM News, CMO.com, BtoB Online, 1to1 Media, Top Sales World, DemandGen Report, Sales and Marketing Management, Sales Lead Management Association, Target Marketing, and The CMO Site;

- well-known national speaker at top industry events, radio shows, and customer conferences;

- current PhD candidate, working on a thesis related to Revenue Marketing;

- Chancellor of Revenue Marketing University—an educational forum run *by* revenue marketing executives *for* revenue marketing leaders;

- Sales Leadership Management Association (SLMA) Top 20 Women to Watch and Top 50 Most Influential People; and a

- visiting professor at William and Mary's Mason School of Business MBA program in Williamsburg, Virginia.

Debbie lives in Atlanta, Georgia, with her husband, two dogs, and one cat. She has two lovely daughters who are engaged in sales and marketing careers. Debbie is an avid reader, CrossFit enthusiast, and hiker on the mountain trails of North Georgia.